GLIMMERS OF GLORY

DISCOVERING GOD MOMENTS IN THE GLOOMY

LISA WILT

Cover photo by Anderson Photography.

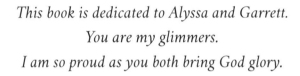

This book is dedicated to Alyssa and Garrett.
You are my glimmers.
I am so proud as you both bring God glory.

ACKNOWLEDGEMENTS

Do you remember what it felt like when the final bell rang on the last day of school signaling the start of summer? The exhilaration. The anticipation. The accomplishment. And how you hooped and hollered with friends feeling so happy and carefree? Together you made it. That's how I feel about my mentors and friends who were so kind to help with this book.

Reverend Mike Costanzo: Even more than your expertise in theology, I value your opinion. God has brought you through the valley of the shadow of death called cancer, so that you can help us all to be more fully alive.

Jonna Beenken and Sue Steen: If there was a class called "Advanced Editing" you both could teach it facing backwards… handcuffed. On the playground of life, I can't think of any friends I would rather have on my team during recess.

My Heavenly Father: When the final bell rings, I'll run to you knowing that heaven will be better than any summer vacation.

A huge THANK YOU to my Glimmers Launch Team: Dawn Anderson, Lynn Arnold, Sharon Baker, Chris Blackburn, Kristen Bomgardner, Rosie Borre, Gail Carlock, Judy Chandler, Kelly Clark, Bee Culver, Lesli Cutshall, Carman Duvall, Traci Dryer, Phyllis Elliott, Bill Ellwood, Amanda Enloe, Cheryl Eustis, Alyssa Falck, Debby Falck, Noel Gorden, Kelly Grissom, Angie Hamilton, Amanda Hanna, Elaine Hanshaw, Janice Harkins, Laura Helton, Patty Hood, Rachel Jensen, Georgia Johnson, Christa Lane, Roxanne Lilly, Ceil Lynch, Natalie Michaels, Therese Nichols, Chris Nees, Kelly Ogle, Luisa Pattison, Janice Reyburn, Mary Rosenquist, Cheyenne Ryberg, Cyndi Scarlett, Kim Shelton, Roxanne Smith, Sue Steen, Billie Sullivan, Shelly Trear, Lisa Trueblood, Doris Vitikani, Anne Wagner, Angie Williams and Diana Wuller.

FORWARD

You may feel **ordinary**, no more special than a solitary droplet of rain in a storm. But I'm here to tell you that you're **extraordinary** in God's eyes. How do I know? God tells us in the first chapter of His Book. After creating you and me, He looks at us and says we are good, "very good" (Genesis 1:31).

As women, we can be so hard on ourselves. We look in the mirror and see our blemishes. You and I look at our lives and see our bent and broken moments. Yet through Christ God looks at us and sees us as His unblemished daughters. He looks at our lives and sees how bent and broken moments can form perfect prisms, allowing us—like colorless light—to be bent and broken, blooming in arcs of color like a rainbow.

Life is a journey through so many seasons. This book shares bent and broken moments from my own journey that started over five decades ago. I was a quiet little girl who grew up in a quiet, little town. Then I left Mattoon and traveled to the loud, large city of St. Louis for pharmacy school. I was bent and broken and my faith was stretched learning about so much more than medicines.

After college I moved to Kansas City, said yes to a job I disliked and "I do" to a man I loved (and still do). Suddenly I found myself in the challenging storm of a turbulent marriage. From two different worlds, Dave and I collided like cold and warm fronts. Trials rained down. Some days I felt we were barely staying afloat. Then God entrusted us first with a daughter then with a son.

Thirty years have passed since then. Alyssa is now grown and shares more in common with me than her smile as she too is a pharmacist. Garrett is following his Dad's footsteps as he studies to become a doctor.

Dave still ministers to his patients working fourteen-hour days as an internal medicine physician. And I continue to work full-time as a pharmacist in industry. Looking back on those early years with young children, I can see how God softened my husband's heart.

The survival of our marriage is a testimony to a flood of answered prayer. Those spring years of marriage and mother-hood brought torrents of rain for sure and I emerged with a heart that cares for women.

We are wives and mothers. Daughters and sisters. Home-makers and coworkers. We have friends and fears...frustrations and flaws. None of us have mastered it all, least of all me, so we need to encourage one another!

In my twenties, God called me to teach Senior High Sunday School. Twenty years later when I hit middle age, God moved me from teaching youth to teaching women. There I continue to find comfort and learn from fellow sojourners.

God has protected me from downpours and poured out His blessings. And He's there, ready and waiting, to bless you too… to provide His umbrella of protection when you feel cold and drenched.

He wants you to do more than survive. He wants you to thrive! And He wants to color your life with **Glimmers of Glory** and show you rainbows after the rains.

INTRODUCTION

THE JOURNEY TO SEE GLIMMERS

The birth of a rainbow begins with a trillion tiny teardrops. These droplets of rain are reflectors of light, providing perfect prisms. Colorless light enters one singular droplet, then exits bent and broken into seven splendid colors of the spectrum. Broken light becomes beautiful and a rainbow is born, blooming in arcs of color!

In my life I have experienced what feels like a trillion tiny trials...gloomy moments for sure. But I've found that these broken moments can become beautiful moments, when I look up to God to see **Glimmers of Glory**.

While rainy days can be gloomy days, I've also learned that rainy days–filled with stormy trials–can also bring vibrant growth. Rain can nourish life, just as trials can nourish faith.

During trials, it's hard to see the complete picture. It's difficult to visualize how God could possibly bring good from the bad we're experiencing. After the storm has passed, can we experience the rainbow?

Did you know that we would see rainbows as complete circles if the earth didn't block the lower half of the arc? There will be a day when our earthly circumstances won't block our eternal vision and we will see the complete picture. Then we will better understand how these trials served to complete us.

For now, since rainbows require only two ingredients — rain and light — I'm starting on a spiritual journey to search for rainbows after the rain. Instead of focusing on the rainy moments, I'm asking God to show me the majestic moments. Those moments that fill us with joy and transform us, so that we can clearly see the good through eyes of faith.

This is my second expectant journey. Last year I so hungered for wonder that I asked God to brighten my day and lighten my load with **W.O.W.** moments–**Windows of Wonder** moments. When I slowed down, God showed up! And when I knelt down, God lifted me up!

Even though my kitchen window was splashed and smudged, God sharpened my spiritual vision on a yearlong adventure, so that I could see Him more clearly. I found extraordinary W.O.W. moments in the ordinary moments of everyday life.

I learned that every day can be a bit more like a holiday when we look to Him to make our lives both whole and holy. So if you need more Light in your life, I know just Who to see.

That's why I'm excited to have you join me on my journey to discover **Glimmers of Glory** in the gloomy moments of everyday life. Will you come along and search for "God moments" nestled between the mounds of bills to be paid and kids to be bathed?

Every morning after we pull up the covers making our beds, we can uncover the unexpected, experiencing His Spirit. We can find more than lost socks in the laundry when we are paired with God. And when we cling to His truths, like socks to a sweater, life becomes sweeter.

Let's ask Him to be our guide every step of the way. And let's depend on His Word for our direction.

When our car keys are misplaced, our cell phones are dead and our gas tanks are on empty, let's turn to God to be refreshed, recharged and refilled.

Like "Chicken Soup for Your Soul," this book is meant to brighten your days. It's lighthearted. There's one chapterette for every day of the month. (Plus a few to spare for those days you need an extra pick-me-up.) It's not meant to be read in one sitting so please don't add it to your already too long list of "to-do's." Heaven knows, you're pulled more directions than a bra that has escaped the lingerie bag in the washer.

Laugh out loud and learn with me as we see how blunders can become blessings. Laughter is good. Breathe deep and exhale purposefully then put on your "Son glasses" and join me on this spiritual search for rainbows after the rain. Let's discover **Glimmers of Glory** not just in the pages of this book but in the stories of our lives.

SWIMMING LESSONS

" *L* ife is difficult." Sound familiar? Although at five I hadn't read *The Road Less Traveled* by Scott Peck, I knew only too well that life had its difficult lessons. Take, for instance, swimming lessons.

Mr. Peck may not have had level one of Red Cross Swimming Lessons in mind when he wrote, but I still remember the slightly slimy concrete as I looked down at my cold, pudgy toes.

My Mom could be as cheerful as she wanted, it didn't change the fact that I was afraid and didn't want to let go of her hand. Other little kids were bustling past me heading straight for the water. I stood like an ice cube frozen to the pavement, partly due to the temperature and partly due to my fear.

Minutes passed. It seemed like hours.

New bathing suit or not, I was unhappy about the arrangement. I saw other children with blue lips from the earlier session shivering toward me, confirming my deepest fears.

I was going to freeze! And my Mom was going to be an accomplice and watch. How could she smile and offer words of encouragement, as I was facing torturous conditions?

Once in the water my knees shook so hard that ringlets rippled in concentric circles around me, as the ruffled skirt on my swimming suit bobbed up and down. But that was the only thing that was going to move!

I was staying where I was…Yes sirree!

Go deeper?

Submerge my face?

Blow bubbles?

NO WAY!

Every muscle in my body had tightened. My jaw clanked. Hairs on my arms stood up in cold defiance. And, oh, the size of those goosebumps!

I was as cold as the banana split my Mom had promised me if I did well. And I was ready to split, heading straight for the nearest exit, which happened to be the boy's locker room.

LIFE IS DIFFICULT: IT'S NEITHER EASY NOR FAIR. AS I WRITE, ONE of the teens in the Sunday school class I teach has lost her nearest cousin of thirteen. He had an asthma attack.

How can someone die from such a common ailment as asthma? Oh, I know the medical answer, but the question I ask is a theological one. How could God allow someone with fewer years than they had fingers and toes to stop breathing?

What would he have become? Where is God in this? All these questions are as valid as the one I had when I was five and as cold and colorful as a blueberry snow cone: "Do I have to do this, Mom?"

The trials and sorrows that we face here on earth are hard...no doubt about it. But just as years have given me some perspective on swimming lessons, years in eternity will give me a different perspective and clear understanding of the questions that I now face.

Amid the frigid and frightening waters of life, I remind myself of Paul's wisdom in Romans 8:38-39:

"And I am convinced that nothing can ever separate
us from God's love.
Neither death nor life, neither angels nor demons,
neither our fears for today nor our worries about tomorrow—
not even the powers of hell can separate us from God's love.
No power in the sky above or in the earth below—
indeed, nothing in all creation will ever be able to separate us
from the love of God that is revealed in Christ Jesus our Lord."

To lose a child is one of the worst possible nightmares for any family. I struggle to understand why God allows the death of children, when He has the power to stop it.

No matter what age a child is when they die, whether they are thirteen or thirty-three, God understands the unfathomable agony. He watched His Only Son die an excruciating, humiliating death that He had the power to stop. As a parent, I struggle to understand this too.

The more years I walk next to my heavenly Father, the more I understand that He is here with me. He walks right alongside me as I struggle through the "valley of the shadow of death" (Psalm 23:4a).

Sometimes the valley looks like a BIG pool to a little girl, who is drowning in fear. Sometimes the valley looks like a dent, a demotion, a divorce…maybe even a death.

Yes. Life is difficult…with deep, cold waters. But heaven will be warm and inviting. And I know our King's rewards will far exceed Dairy Queen's banana split!

THE JOURNEY FORWARD:

At five I was fearful and shivered at the thought of swimming lessons. Now I'm grateful my mother insisted I learn to swim. As a mother myself, I better understand her wisdom. I know that my lessons at Lytle Pool served a higher purpose. Can you read Psalm 69, highlighting it for easy access in times of "deep waters"?

A POOL TABLE OR A PARKING LOT?

*I*t's every mother's nightmare. The phone call that comes with the news that your teenager has been involved in a car crash. One Saturday when I was in high school, my Mom received that alarming call.

Ironically, it was the first time I had ever taken the car out of town by myself. Heading home from a *Teen's Encounter with Christ* Reunion, my front passenger tire got stuck in the rut where Route 16 had been widened and patched. Being an inexperienced highway driver, I overcorrected at 60 m.p.h. and started to swerve uncontrollably.

A family sedan barreled straight toward me. To my right was a deep ravine and beyond it a railroad track that ran parallel to the highway. To my left was a new car dealership. I careened into the lot, narrowly escaping a head-on collision.

Like a billiard ball on a pool table, my car crashed into five colorful new trucks all lined up on the front row of the Ford dealership just outside Pana, Illinois.

Until that day, I had never visited a new car lot and didn't realize that the most expensive vehicles are kept in the front row. I took out five trucks first, then two cars, before I spun out and stalled. I landed beside a white sedan that was much nicer than my family's green Maverick. It had no power steering, no power windows and no air-conditioning. It now looked like a crumpled 7-Up can.

I was dazed and bruised but had no broken bones. The driver's side door wouldn't open, so I tumbled out the passenger side. The dealership owner ran toward me absolutely thrilled to have sold seven vehicles in seven seconds.

His response was exuberant; I was mortified at the mess I had made. Those who were eating in the restaurant next door began to file out to see the wreckage. The owner laughed as I limped to his office so that I could use his phone to call my parents. Cell phones didn't exist back then.

I told my Mom where I was, but I omitted a few details–seven large damaged details to be exact. As I waited for my parents, I looked at the totaled vehicles and totaled their sticker prices.

People kept asking me if I was okay. I was more concerned about the vehicles I had damaged than the damage to my left shoulder and hip. I just kept thinking that my college tuition lay scattered before me.

A policeman arrived, asked if I was fine, then handed me a fine (a fifty-dollar ticket). He requested my insurance papers.

Until that moment, I had never thought about insurance. So when the officer insisted on proof of my policy, I panicked. I should've known that even though money was tight, my father–forever the good provider working three jobs–had good insurance. Dad had me covered.

The irony was that my father drove a truck he bought for fifty dollars from Mr. Tucker–a man we knew from church. Jack planned to sell it to the junkyard, but Dad rescued the old truck and named her "Old Gold."

Her floor was rusted out, so we could see the highway whiz by under our feet. Dad called it "her air-conditioning." My mother called her "a death trap." Mom was concerned the cab might detach from the bed. While Old Gold was once gold, she was more rust-colored now.

Dad loved that truck because she was "a good ole' bargain." He nursed another decade from her by replacing her engine. With a tight budget for a family of five and with college being a priority, a new vehicle was never a luxury he could afford.

My Dad always said: "New cars make poor investments." You can imagine what a surprise it was for him to pick up his middle child in the middle of a wrecked-up car lot. I was so sorry.

The bruises lasted a few weeks.

The embarrassment lasted a few years.

And the nerves that sometimes grip me when driving on the highway have lasted a few decades. To this day I wouldn't describe myself as a confident driver.

❧

ARE THERE TIMES IN YOUR LIFE WHEN YOU NEED TO BE PICKED UP
and rescued? For me, this was one of those gloomy times. I was
a puddle of tears. My Dad was a pillar of strength.

He spoke confidently to the police officer, who tore up the
ticket and handed him the pieces. Then we climbed into Old
Gold with me sandwiched between my loving parents and
headed home to Mattoon.

Anyone who knows my Dad knows that he has quite a sense
of humor, but that day he didn't crack any corny jokes. He knew
I was badly shaken. When I apologized for demolishing the
family car, he was complimentary saying: "Well, sweetheart,
when you do something, you always go all in."

My Mom prayed out loud, thanking God for my safety.
When we finally arrived home, I was so bruised and stiff that I
could barely walk; my Grandma was waiting to welcome me.
From that day forward she would always greet me with a hug
and kiss reminding me: "Lisa, God spared you for a purpose."

Many years have passed and I have driven many miles acci-
dent-free. Today I remember the day my Dad rescued me. Today
also happens to be Super Bowl Sunday.

This morning my pastor, a sports fan and an even bigger fan
of Jesus, spoke of football and redemption during his sermon.
He commemorated the historic comeback and Super Bowl win
by the Patriots. Pastor Mike explained that sixty-five percent of
the time, the first team to score wins the big game.

However, in 2017, in the **third** quarter the Patriots were
behind by twenty-three points. Even still they went on to defeat

the Redskins in overtime, which had never been seen before in Super Bowl history.

The Patriots were "redeemed" just when their faithful followers thought all had been lost and it was over. Then Pastor Mike pointed out the connection. When Jesus was crucified–and when His followers thought all was lost and it was over–on the third day Jesus came back and redeemed us.

Like the Patriots defeated the Redskins, Jesus defeated sin and death. While I don't follow football, I did follow Pastor Mike's message. He shared that no words can adequately capture the depth of love God has for us to send His Son to die for our sins.

He shared the John 3:16 football-fan-favorite Scripture that frequently is waved on poster board:

> "For this is how God loved the world:
> He gave his one and only Son,
> so that everyone who believes in him
> will not perish but have eternal life."

Then he read St. Paul's words, which remind us that God bought us for a high price (1 Corinthians 6:20). Finally Pastor Mike quoted Matthew 20:28:

> "For even the Son of Man came not to be served
> but to serve others and to give his life as a ransom for many."

So in each of these three verses, St. John, St. Paul and even

Jesus describe His sacrifice a bit differently: redeemed, bought and ransomed. Each help us comprehend the magnitude of the gift of salvation.

Pastor Mike concluded his sermon celebrating this gift of grace with communion. The bread and wine remind us of Christ's body and blood offered for the atonement of the sins of all humankind. Closing the service he asked us to reflect on examples of redemption from our own lives.

As we sang the last hymn, my thoughts drifted to the day my earthly father redeemed me...the day I played billiards with the family sedan in a colorful car lot.

I couldn't afford a vehicle.

I couldn't afford insurance.

I could barely afford a tank of gas.

And while I may have deserved a ticket for reckless driving, my earthly father saw things differently through eyes of grace. And for that I am grateful. Now years later looking back, I see **Glimmers of Glory** in this gloomy moment.

But the story gets even better. Two years after my heavenly Father spared my life, my earthly father filled Old Gold with my earthly possessions. Dad moved me from the little city of Mattoon to the big city of St. Louis, where I attended pharmacy school.

Years later when I took my first job as a community pharmacist, I made more annually than my dad had ever made. He worked for the Mattoon Street Department full-time, owned rental properties and sold siding on the side.

A few years later when I was financially on my feet, I took

my Dad to a new car lot and bought him a shiny, blue truck to replace rusty Old Gold. He adorned his new truck with the personalized license plate–"Gift 95"–to remember the year he had his first new vehicle. He was sixty-one then.

THE JOURNEY FORWARD:

When you think of God's gift of redemption through Jesus, do you remember a time when you were touched by grace... a time when someone saved you from a mess you had made, extending love instead of judgement? If so, grace has *colored* your life.

Which brings me back to the *colorful* billiard balls and my father...have you ever told the person who rescued you how much you appreciate them? If not, might you reach out to them today?

SNAPPY SERVICE

Growing up, my big sister and I loved to play with bubbles, making all sorts of imaginary creations out of suds. One of our favorite games we called "Snappy Service." It was our fictitious, fast-food joint we ran out of our playhouse that was as big as most sheds and conveniently positioned outside my Mom's kitchen window.

Our playhouse was white and delicately trimmed in red scallops, which my dad made "pretty like his two girls." Inside we had a hand-powered mixer, lots of Styrofoam® containers and even more imagination.

I would take the food requests from my little brother, who would obediently pedal past the "drive-up window" on his tricycle to place his order. My friend, Susie Stuckey, would come up the alley to join in the wet fun.

We spent countless hours swirling, whirling and sudsing our

way through sizzling, summer days. Our goal was to make as many bubbles as fast as we possibly could. We strove to be snappy when making our soapy concoctions. But the frustrating property of bubbles is that after you stop whipping them, they slowly disappear.

EVEN THOUGH I'M AN ADULT NOW AND STILL ENJOY PLAYING WITH bubbles alongside my kiddos, some days I find myself in a bustle of bubbly busyness, like scrubbing sinks and scouring surfaces to make them sparkle.

But I become so busy, I don't stop to catch my breath. And I certainly don't have time to rest at the feet of Jesus and learn from Him. No sirree. There are mounds of meals to be made and loads of laundry to be…well…laundered…and folded…and sorted…and put neatly away only to start over the next day.

It's as if I'm nine again and caught in a long summer daze playing Snappy Service. I keep whipping the water in a frenzy, because I know if I don't the suds will dissolve and my hard work will disappear. Then my house will become a hot mess. (Gasp!)

Recently I was reminded of dissolving bubbles and Snappy Service, when I was reading a passage from **2 Peter 3:10-12. It speaks of Christ's glorious return, when the temporary things of Earth will be "dissolved." Knowing that this world is fleeting, St. Peter asks:

"What kind of person should you be?"

God touched my weary heart in that glimmering moment. He silently whispered through His Word for me to stop *whisking* and start *resting*.

To sit with Him.

To pause in my journey.

To look to Him for **Glimmers of Glory.**

To refresh and renew me. And then I remembered a story from the Bible that's found in Luke 10:38-42. In four short verses, we encounter two women. One was short-tempered, short on help and short on time. She was caught in a game of Snappy Service. We find her "worried and upset." The other we find resting, learning at the feet of our Lord. We read in verses 40-42:

"Martha was distracted by the big dinner she was preparing.
She came to Jesus and said, 'Lord, doesn't it seem unfair to you
that my sister just sits here while I do all the work?
Tell her to come and help me.' But the Lord said to her,
'My dear Martha, you are worried and upset over these details!
There is only one thing worth being concerned about.
Mary has discovered it, and it will not be taken away from her.'"

Mary had discovered what was most important and wasn't caught in the game of Snappy Service. Jesus reaffirms both her and her journey.

As I sat with my Bible, now closed on my lap, I knew an

uncluttered house was not the most essential thing but rather an *uncluttered heart* that is focused on Christ.

And therein lies the secret and the **Glimmer of Glory**. A heart focused on Christ is not overcome, "worried and upset" in serving.

Yes. Our families will still grow hungry and need to be fed. Dirty clothes will still fill our hampers, but our hearts won't be hampered because the difference between service that is *fleeting* and service that is *focused* is the heart attitude.

Service done in love…

in His name…

to extend His grace…

for others…

not to make ourselves look good.

These acts of loving service will never dissolve like bubbles. The impact is eternal. How do I know? It's a truth that I learned in 1 Corinthians 13:13. Here St. Paul concludes his chapter on love, saying:

> "Three things will last forever
> —faith, hope and love—
> and the greatest of these is love."

It's simple, but eternally profound. God is love (1 John 4:8).

Good golly. Sometimes I make my life more complicated and busier than it needs to be. If you and I love God and then love others, we have done everything that He asks of us (Matthew

22:37-38). And we are living a life that brings God immense glory.

THE JOURNEY FORWARD:

On your journey forward, let God encourage you through **M &
M**'s–not the candies (that I crave) but the two sisters named
Martha and **M**ary. If you pour water today to wash dishes, can
you be reminded that, unlike bubbles, love lasts forever? Might
you take time today to love God as Mary did through quiet
adoration, learning at His feet?

SCATTERING THE LIGHT

This morning my sweet, inquisitive Alyssa asked me a question as she wondered out loud, "Momma, why is the sky blue?"

We were on an all-out sprint to the store to buy fresh hamburger buns for our barbecue and I was struggling to unbuckle my son from his impossible car seat. Honestly, I had forgotten why the sky was blue. In haste, I had also forgotten my grocery list on the kitchen counter. Good grief.

"I think blue might be God's favorite color," I retorted. "Like Daddy's."

Later that afternoon, when tummies were full and eyes were napping, I looked up the answer online.[1] I learned that the sky is blue for the same reason that large bodies of water are blue. The color is caused by the scattering of sunlight. If it were not for this scattering, the day sky would appear as dark as the night sky and large bodies of water would appear black.

While snorkeling is about my speed, if you've done any deep-sea diving, you know that the deeper you dive, the less light there is to be scattered resulting in a shroud of darkness. Unlike the depths of the oceans, the night sky is never completely dark because the earth's atmosphere also scatters light from stars and galaxies.

When you're flying at lower altitudes, you may have noticed that the sky is lighter because the atmosphere is thicker (resulting in more scattering). At higher altitudes, the sky is darker because the atmosphere is thinner (resulting in less scattering).

This also explains why outer space is dark, even though it's closer to the sun. Honestly, when I'm stuck on a plane, I'm sometimes more preoccupied with how slow the snack cart seems to be making its way to my seat. Nevertheless, God's glory and this phenomenon of light being scattered exists outside the plane window.

Today I learned the amount of scattering caused by atoms and molecules depends strongly on the wavelength of the light. Shorter wavelengths scatter more light. As a result, the short wavelength or blue component of sunlight tends to be scattered in all directions.

The long wavelength appears red. It tends to travel in straight lines. For this reason, light coming directly from the sun contains less blue and appears redder than it would be if there were no scattering. This is why we tend to think of the sun's glimmering rays as being red rather than blue. Does this ring true to you?

Dust particles and water droplets, which are much larger than single molecules, scatter both the light of longer and shorter wavelengths in nearly equal amounts. Thus, the light scattered by these particles cancel each other out, appearing white. We call these masses of particles and water clouds. Boy, have you forgotten as much as I had since middle school science?

THESE FACTS MADE ME THINK. JUST AS ATOMS AND MOLECULES scatter sunlight to illuminate the atmosphere and give large bodies of water color, aren't we as Christians called to scatter the light of Christ? This too illuminates the world "coloring" the face of the earth.

Without atoms and molecules, the sky wouldn't exist as we know it. Likewise, without God's people sharing the love of Christ, the world wouldn't exist as we know it.

We each have a role in scattering the Light. You and I each make a difference. The church is as diverse as atoms, molecules and water droplets found in the sky. Just as each of these components of our atmosphere scatter sunlight differently, each of us has a different role and mission to accomplish for Christ. We learn in 1 Corinthians 12:4-6:

"There are different kinds of service,

but we serve the same Lord.

God works in different ways,

but it is the same God who does the work in all of us."

We each scatter His Light differently, just as the particles of our atmosphere scatter light differently. No one color is better than another and no one role, work or service in the church is better than another, deserving more attention.

We each work together to give the world the Light—the message of salvation. Likewise, each component of the atmosphere together scatter light, coloring the sky and ocean. We have so much to learn on this journey. Together might we live these truths?

THE JOURNEY FORWARD:

Pour yourself water in a clear glass. Notice that the water lacks color. Yet that one small glassful, when poured into the ocean, appears blue. Likewise you may feel that your efforts to scatter the Light of Christ providing colorful hope are futile, but be encouraged. Together we can make a difference. You and I can color the face of the earth as we scatter the Light of our Savior! Let's transform gloomy moments into glimmering moments with kindness.

---

1. *NASA Space Place "Why is the Sky Blue" NASA.gov* https://spaceplace.nasa.gov/blue-sky/en/ (Accessed March 3, 2019.)

BARNEY BLUE BELL

KING OF THE WILD FRONTIER

When my brother was a preschooler, we called him Barney Blue Bell. Brian just looked like a Barney; he loved his well-worn overalls coupled with his comfy cowboy boots.

His other love was keys, which made him feel very important. My father welded a huge, metal ring so that every old key we would find could be clipped to Barney's overall strap. He jingled when he walked. This too made him feel very grownup.

Barney's third love was drinking pop–a special treat at the Nale household, as it was unwholesome. The pop man, who filled the vending machines, had lots of pop and lots of keys. So Barney dreamed of being a pop man when he grew up.

On special occasions my Dad would give Barney a shiny dime and together they would make the exciting trip to visit the vending machines. Barney loved to place his coin in the slot, hearing it clink as it fell and seeing the can obediently drop down into the tray.

He and Dad would sit with their drink in front of the Mattoon Street Department and watch cars drive by on Richmond Avenue. Sometimes they would sing a tune together about Barney Blue Bell, who became King of the Wild Frontier.

Brian loved time spent with my Dad...as much as he disliked clothes shopping with my Mom. He was prone to wander off during shopping expeditions. Such was the case when we went to K-Mart for the Back-to-School sale.

In our quaint town in the early 70's, there was little concern of Brian being kidnapped. Everyone knew each other for the most part. But when a clerk saw that he was lost and didn't recognize to whom he belonged, she asked his name.

With a quivering bottom lip, Brian looked up at her with big, blue eyes and answered, "Barney Blue Bell." When she asked for his last name, he replied "King of the Wild Frontier."

Oh my...I wish I could have seen the look on her face as she peered down at Barney, a distressed four-year-old dressed in threadbare overalls. He sniffled when he offered, "My mommy was just at the jewdry counter."

Mom and I were now looking for shoes not far from the jewelry department, when we heard over the loud speaker: "If you've lost a blonde boy in overalls, he's waiting for you up front at the Service Desk."

Simultaneously shocked, we both looked at each other and headed straight for Customer Service. When we arrived, there was Barney with his big key ring and a big grin, so relieved to see faces he knew.

Holding his hand was a lady with an equally big grin. She explained: "He said his name was 'Barney Blue Bell–King of the Wild Frontier.'" After that, my Mom asked my Dad to stop calling him "Barney Blue Bell, King of the Wild Frontier" and start emphasizing that his name was, in fact, Brian Nale. She wanted him to be prepared for kindergarten next year.

MY SON'S NAME IS GARRETT REMINGTON DAVID WILT. WHEN HE hears all four names, he instinctively knows he's in trouble! Today I was teaching him to say his full name. He has Garrett down pat. But "Remington" is a bit more difficult. I repeat it slowly, emphasizing each syllable.

I ask him to repeat after me: "Rem-ing-ton."

Each time he diligently offers: "Rum-me-tum."

It's so cute. He even rubs his rounded cherub's tummy for added emphasis. I can't help but giggle.

We sometimes have pet names for family members. In knowing Christ, we become part of God's family. I wonder if He'll call us by our formal names or our nicknames?

Though my formal name is Elizabeth, I've always gone by Lisa. I didn't answer to Elizabeth, nor did I know how to spell it in kindergarten. This created quite the confusion during roll call that first day at St. Mary's School.

Today we tend to choose names based on how they sound,

rather than on their meaning. However, in Biblical times, the name your parents gave you was most often a family name, which had greater significance.

Likewise, the names that God and Jesus changed were altered for a reason. In Genesis we can read about Abram becoming Abraham. [1]In the Hebrew language Abram means "high father."

The name Abraham, however, means "father of a multitude." God changed Abraham's name based on the covenant, that he would become more than a high father; he would become the father of a multitude–an entire nation (Genesis 17:5).

Likewise, Sarai's name means "dominative."[2] It's the female derivative of "a head person." Although Sarah is taken from the same root, it means "lady, princess, queen." Sarah was blessed and enriched with her new name.

There is both rhyme and reason to God's actions. Later in Genesis we meet Jacob, whose name means "deceiver." With the help of his mom, Rebekah, Jacob deceived his dad, Isaac, for his brother Esau's birthright (Genesis 27).

But the tables turn when five chapters later "the deceiver" was deceived by his father-in-law and uncle, Laben. He was duped into marrying the wrong daughter, Leah, who had "weak eyes" (Genesis 29).

This is quite ironic since Jacob, who had strong vision, was deceived by his true love's sister, who had poor vision. Jacob was reaping what he sowed, which is a principle of God's kingdom (Hosea 10:12).

Then we can read about how Jacob wrestled with God. After

this encounter, Jacob limped, relying on a staff to walk. Symbolic of his need and willingness to now lean on God, Jacob's name was changed to "Israel," meaning "he will rule as God" (Genesis 32:28).

In Matthew 1:21, Joseph was explicitly told by the angel, Gabriel, to name Mary's son, Jesus. In the Greek language, Jesus means "the name of our Lord." In the Hebrew language, Jesus is another name for Jehoshua or Joshua. Both were very common names in Biblical times.

Jesus is also called our Lord Jesus Christ. While Christ does sound like a last name or surname, it is not. Christ is Greek for "Christos" which means "anointed one" or "chosen one." This is the Greek equivalent of the Hebrew word "Messiah."

While "Jesus" is the Lord's human name, "Christ" is His title, signifying Jesus was sent from God to be a King and Deliverer. "Jesus Christ" means "Jesus the Messiah" or "Jesus the Anointed One."[3]

THE JOURNEY FORWARD:

My brother–Brian Nale–has outgrown both his overalls and his nickname of Barney Blue Bell. Likewise we each do change and mature over time. On your journey forward, what new name would fit your new identity in Christ?

As a woman who has a heart for serving other women, I can relate to a lady named Dorcas. (Yes. I can be a bit of a dork too so the name fits.) She had a touching ministry that you can read about in Acts 9:36-42.

Is there someone in Scripture with whom you can relate on a personal level? Do you share similar personalities or qualities with them? God made you glimmer...to bring Him Glory!

---

1. My Scripture-nary Online. s.v. "Abram/Abraham" June 9, 2019. http://www.thekeyofknowledge.net/Religion/I_Define.html
2. My Scripture-nary Online. s.v. "Sarai/Sarah" June 9, 2019. http://www.thekeyofknowledge.net/Religion/I_Define.html
3. Strong's Concordance Online. s.v. "Jesus" March 3, 2019 Biblehub.com https://biblehub.com/greek/2424.html

DADDY'S GLASSES

AND THE LIBRARY OF COMPARISON

*M*oments ago my daughter walked to my desk wearing her Daddy's glasses and shared: "These make me dizzy." Then she smiled adding: "And I can't see you too good either." But to my surprise, she didn't want to take them off.

It's one of the many disorienting pleasures that children enjoy...much like turning around and around in circles until they can't stand up. As she bumped into walls, I walked her back down the hallway. Then we turned into the bedroom to put my husband's glasses back on his nightstand, where she had found them.

Once back at my desk, I was left to reflect on how often we mirror Alyssa's actions. We see someone we admire and then we "wear their glasses" in an effort to resemble them.

When I was young, I remember wanting to mirror my Mom.

As I became a teenager, I wanted to mirror the fashion and hair-styles of those I saw on TV and in magazines.

In my early twenties I developed my own style, accenting my better features while deemphasizing my flaws. In short, it took me time to learn what was best left to the models and movie stars. Now it's fun to look back and laugh at pictures of me growing up in the seventies and eighties with big bell bottoms and even bigger hair.

As we mature into adults, we're a bit less likely to outwardly duplicate everything we see. Ah...but are we totally free from the perils of comparison?

Perhaps we're more subtle, but we still have to guard against looking at others and taking notes of comparison. As women, we can be hard on ourselves. Wouldn't you agree?

We take mental notes on others' appearance. In fact, we have complete volumes on beauty shelved in our brains like books in a library. We have written mental books of comparison...

on skin...

on smiles...

on styles...

on pant and shirt sizes...

on hair colors and styles.

We have an entire wing of the library of our minds crammed full of critiques on our figures. While we may be gentle with others, we are unkind–even cruel–with our own self-critiques. I find that we have perfected the Dewey Decimal System when it comes to classifying beauty.

And we don't stop there. Aside from beauty we have rooms

in our mental library dedicated to relationships. We have encyclopedic-sized collections of comparisons about our spouses. Just as encyclopedias are alphabetized and have pictures, we document the shortcomings of our mate and take mental pictures so we dare not forget the times they didn't live up to our expectations.

Our expectations are often established by what we perceive, based on Facebook posts of other couples. We take note of how often their spouse surprises them with flowers. Thus we begin authoring our own encyclopedias with outrageous expectations.

A is for Affection. Spouses must publicly display affection toward us.

B is for Beautiful. Spouses must think we are beyond beautiful and tell us everyday…regardless of our raccoon remnants of mascara from yesterday.

C is for Captivating. Spouses must be captivating keeping our attention emotionally, physically and spiritually.

We seek perfection, being disappointed and disenchanted when others seem to have their "happily ever after."

There is row after row dedicated to our children, comparing their school success, stability and sports skills to those of our friends' kids.

And speaking of friends, we have limited edition collections of those too. We keep microfiche files on failed friendships and prior coworkers. In short, we compare the number and quality of our friendships to those we see on Facebook. It's cyber silliness.

And while online, we archive mental notes on home décor and

pin them (sometimes even from Pinterest) to the bulletin boards in our mental libraries. We critique our aptitude for homemaking, compare our cooking abilities, contrast our gardening skills, categorize our home's organization and consider our basic tidiness.

And I haven't even mentioned the entire floor of our mind's library that is dedicated to our wedding memories. We compare:

dresses,

decorations,

locations,

entertainment,

entrees,

themes,

pictures, *and*

cakes...or lack thereof!

Oh...and the ring. Yes, the ring. We compare the size of the stone, the style of the setting and the color of the gold. Which brings me to our grooms, who gave us the ring.

While our men may not compare and value the same things that we do, they too are vulnerable to comparison. While we compare our physical beauty and the beauty surrounding our lives and relationships, they compare their physical and financial strength.

They take mental notes on the size of

their investment portfolios...

their savings...

their cars...

the size of the engines in their cars...

the size of their homes...

and the size and number of the TV's in those homes.

They build their mental libraries of comparison by the rules that:

- "Bigger is better."
- "BIG boys have BIG toys." And...
- "He who dies with the most toys wins."

Being a librarian to our brain's critiques is mentally taxing. And I haven't even taken the elevator to the top floor of the library that houses all our spiritual comparisons.

We have sections that compare our ministries to the outreach of others. Secluded private cubicles that compare our Biblical knowledge, our prayer lives, our church attendance, our journaling skills and our tithing. Compilations that record our faithfulness—both past and present.

Dustiest of all, we each have areas of our library that are "closed to the public." We have internalized comments from years gone by as if they were yesterday; we keep those in the audiovisual room of our mental library. Some weeks we replay them over and over.

COMPARISON CAN CREEP INTO EVERY CORNER OF OUR MINDS LIKE dust can creep into every corner of the library. While we can learn from others' lives of faith, we are wisest when we strive to be like Christ. He alone was perfect (Hebrews 5:8-9).

We are lovingly cautioned in Romans 12:2:

"Don't copy the behavior and customs of this world,
but let God transform you into a new person
by changing the way you think.
Then you will learn to know God's will for you,
which is good and pleasing and perfect."

Practically speaking, how do we clean the dust of comparison out of our minds so we can be transformed? We learn exactly how in Hebrews 12:1-2:

"Strip off everything that slows us down...
And let us run with endurance the race God has set before us.
We do this by keeping our eyes on Jesus,
the champion who initiates and perfects our faith."

To paraphrase Paul loosely, we need to shake off the dust of comparison that tends to settle on us, looking to Christ as our dust-free, shining example. He will help us run the race perfecting our faith.

In Biblical times runners would quite literally strip down to their birthday suits, so that they could sprint without the extra weight of clothing. While I wouldn't want to shock my neighbors and run naked, I certainly could lose the emotional burden of comparison.

Paul understands the issues and tells us that he's not trying to win the approval of people, but of God. He says that if pleasing people were his goal, he wouldn't be Christ's servant (Galatians 1:10).

Which brings us back to the all-important question. What is our overarching goal…to please ourselves and others or to please God?

May I share a personal weakness with you? By nature I'm a people-pleaser. I don't like to disappoint others. When I think others are upset with me, I can lose sleep. Interestingly, I married a man who hasn't lost a moment's rest because he's concerned over what others think.

If I truly lived the truth penned by Paul, I could clean out my comparison library. I would sleep better, knowing that I only need to please Christ. How about you? Is your deepest desire to please Jesus and reflect Him?

Paul embraces differences. To use his analogy found in *Romans 12:5-6, we each have a different role in the body of Christ. If we are called to be part of the hand, we need to be the best hand we can be:

> "Let's just go ahead and be what we were made to be,
> without enviously or pridefully
> **comparing ourselves with each other**,
> or trying to be something we aren't."

With this in mind, I ask myself routinely throughout my week and before I commit to new responsibilities: "Am I motivated by the desire to be bring God Glory?" This question keeps me God-focused.

We each have different talents. You may be great at organizing church functions, while others may be terrific teachers. Some may be better at balancing the church's finances, while others would be miserable working with numbers (Ahem...that's me).

Though we all have different strengths and weaknesses, we each have a role. The important lesson is that we don't try to "wear each others' glasses," as it can distort our vision and disorient us, as it did my sweet daughter.

THE JOURNEY FORWARD:

On your journey forward, rather than comparing yourself to others trying to resemble them, mirror Christ and His example of serving. What do you excel at and what do you enjoy doing?

Are you using these talents to bring others **Glimmers of Glory**? If not, might you pray that God would give you His vision for your life and ministry?

MRS. MOBERLY

PAIN AND THE PIANO

*M*rs. Moberly was my piano teacher when I was in grade school. Everything about her was old. She was cold and gritty too, not at all like my Grandma, who was warm and loving.

Mrs. Moberly was a bony, abnormally tall woman with wiry, gray hair and brittle, ashen skin. The whites of her eyes were yellow. I never remember seeing her smile or laugh.

She lived in a worn-out apartment that would have been bare had it not been for her baby grand. It was her *late* husband's piano. She spoke of him often. It seemed odd to me that she would keep calling him late when he was dead.

I could sense she was lonely but she seemed to like me, so I tried to like her too. Really she frightened me in a foreboding sort of way. It was strange to feel both sorry for someone and scared of them at the same time. I would tremble with terror at the thought of her being disappointed in me.

Remove the "o," shuffle the vowels and "piano" spells "pain." Anything that shortened the pain of piano lessons, I welcomed. Once my sister accidentally rode over my head as if it were a speed bump, after I fell biking home from the mall. My Mom thought my face would be bloodied, but I just bloodied my knee and was no worse for wear.

On the way home we stopped at the Prudential Insurance building to use the drinking fountain. My Mom thoughtfully wiped the blood dripping down my leg, then we headed out the heavy, metal double doors. That's when the unthinkable happened. My hand was crushed in the door. Each swollen finger throbbed much worse than my head ached.

Although I had a long welt from the tire on the back of my head, a skinned knee and giant knuckles, I had a huge smile on my face! Why? My Mom said I wouldn't have to go to piano lessons the next day.

Mrs. Moberly was a disciplinarian, holding me accountable for my musical development. The result was easy to hear. I played Chopin and Beethoven beautifully with proper technique and timing.

Sadly, I never enjoyed playing. While my hands obeyed, my heart didn't sing. As soon as my parents stopped insisting that I go, I rarely ever sat down to "tickle the ivory." And I never saw Mrs. Moberly again.

So why am I remembering Mrs. Moberly today as I sit at my computer keyboard? When I type a letter incorrectly, it sometimes reminds me of playing the wrong key on the piano. Though decades have passed, I still hear Mrs. Moberly's voice.

So as we journey forward looking for **Glimmers of Glory** in the gloomy moments, I think of her. Mrs. Moberly was certainly gloomy. Even more than being gloomy, she was downright gritty.

Have you had someone in your life who was like Mrs. Moberly? Maybe they were an aunt or uncle, a coach or teacher. And maybe the "gritty" approach worked to engage both your head and your heart. For me, discipline devoid of love only led me to dislike the piano.

Maybe the gritty person is still in your life. I have a gritty person who plays a major role in mine. While gritty people may be disciplined and hardworking, earning my respect in many ways, there are times when they hurt my heart.

Would you agree that being gritty can be both good and bad? As we journey forward, this brings me to God. Some people see God as gritty.

There are certainly aspects of God from the Old Testament that can sound gritty, even harsh. But the more I come to know the complete heart of God, the more I see His love for us.

I have come to know Him best through His Son. In Romans 8:15, Paul shares that we have not:

"received a spirit that makes you fearful slaves.
Instead, you received God's Spirit

when he adopted you as his own children.
Now we call him, 'Abba, Father.'"

Abba means Father. When I pray to God, I start my conversations with "Abba." How do you address God when you pray?

God wants you to talk to Him and He wants you to know that He loves you! St. Paul is adamant in Romans 8:37-38, sharing:

"neither death, nor life, nor angels, nor principalities,
nor powers, nor things present, nor things to come,
nor height, nor depth, nor any other creature,
shall be able to separate us from the love of God."

I can rest secure in that love. I never rested secure in anything when it came to the piano. St. John knew the heart of Jesus. He tells us that perfect love "casts out" all fear (1 John 4:18).

John was filled with love and He was fearless. He was Mrs. Moberly's age when he was exiled to a gloomy, gritty pit on the island of Patmos where he penned this truth. He was a wise, gentle, elderly man who had experienced God's love for nearly eight decades. It had smoothed and softened his jagged, bellowing heart.

As a young man, you might remember that he was called a "Son of Thunder" along with his brother, James. Back then he was loud and gritty, but love transformed him. Now his old heart was tranquil. He prayed with the calming confidence of a child of God.

Yes. There are many Scriptures that talk about "the fear of God." We are told in Psalm 128:1:

> "How joyful are those who fear the Lord
> –all who follow his ways!"

So the verse defines those who "fear the Lord" as those who "follow his ways." Even today when someone is described as a "God-fearing person" we understand them to be moral, following God's commandments.

When I read God's Word, I use a New Living Translation, Learning Application Bible that often translates the word "fear" as "reverence." Certainly God deserves our reverence…even our obedience.

But God doesn't want *fearful* obedience; He invites us to experience *joyful* obedience. This leads to freedom. He knows that sin enslaves people. Obedience can free people.

God is all-powerful, but His power is beautifully balanced with unending love. Out of this love He wants us to obey, so that we can avoid the pain that sin brings to us and those we love.

I believe St. John understood this when he emphasized that we should love one another. He said that love comes from God and anyone who is a child of God should love others (1 John 4:7-8).

He wants us to come to Him as His children because we love

Him, not because we're fearful of Him. He doesn't want us to dread Him.

This brings me full circle back to Mrs. Moberly, who would scold me when I played a wrong note. She wasn't able to express love freely. Because I couldn't relate to her gritty edges, I was fearful.

Please know that God wants to connect with you, so much that He sent His Only Son to us here on earth. And when Jesus went back home to heaven, He sent His Spirit, the Comforter.

How do you need to be comforted today? Whether you are a nine-year-old learning Mozart's sonatas on a baby grand or a ninety-year-old learning to text your grandkids on a smartphone, know that you are not alone. And please know that you are dearly loved.

THE JOURNEY FORWARD:

As an adult looking back, I understand that my parents' intentions were good, wanting to introduce me to music. And I believe Mrs. Moberly's intentions were good too, as she taught the only way she knew how. Nevertheless, the result for me was that playing the piano was devoid of joy.

On your journey forward today, can you ask God to heal a gloomy, gritty memory that is devoid of joy? He wants you to bask in the beauty of Philippians 4:9:

> "God, who makes everything work together,
> **will work you into his most excellent harmonies.**"

DOGGONE DICKEY

*D*o you own a dickey? Or do you, like many others, have no earthly idea what a dickey could possibly be? Mr. Webster defines it as a "false shirt front." It's a partial article of clothing that can't be worn by itself. Growing up I had a turtleneck dickey that I wore in the neckline of a jumper.

Now that we all know what dickeys are, I have a dilemma and I need your advice. What would you do if you were in my shoes? Here's your chance to, like King Solomon, listen to a saga and impart your wisdom.

It's the case of the missing dickey!

One of the dozens of volunteers who graciously offered their time and talent when I commissioned them to wrap Christmas presents for charity became quite warm in his elf-like haste. He removed the dickey from his collar, laying it at the end of the table near the gifts to be wrapped.

It was a congested area with a flurry of activity. You can only guess what happened. When his shift was over, he went to find his dickey. Despite a concerted effort by all involved, it had vanished like Santa's sleigh into the starry sky.

Where would you guess the dickey could've gone? If you think that some well-meaning volunteer had wrapped it up, we're reading off the same hymnal. What would you have done if you were me coordinating the event?

Would you have disregarded the distress of a valuable volunteer? Might you have unwrapped several dozen gifts in one last effort to retrieve the dickey? I was perplexed... and did neither.

However, I did politely offer to buy the gentleman a new dickey. He declined. The real disappointment was yet to come as some expectant tot tore open their package on Christmas morning, only to find–yep, you guessed it–a doggone dickey.

HIDDEN IN THE DILEMMA OF THE DISAPPEARING DICKEY THERE IS A lesson to be unwrapped. As people we have much in common with this dickey. Not only are we lost (like the dickey) before we come to know Christ as Savior, but we too are incomplete.

In accepting Christ, we are accepting the call to be "followers of Christ." So in order to become like Him, we are called to learn more about Him. His Living Word reveals His true nature. In 2 Timothy 3:16-17, St. Paul explains:

"All Scripture is inspired by God

and is useful to teach us what is true and
to make us realize what is wrong in our lives.
It corrects us when we are wrong
and teaches us to do what is right.
God uses it to prepare and equip his people
to do every good work."

The King James Version of this verse tells us that Scripture allows us to be *thoroughly* equipped and perfectly complete, lacking nothing.

Unlike a dickey, God wants us to be more than just what a person sees on the outside. He wants us to be *thoroughly* clothed with good works. He doesn't want us to be fake.

And He certainly doesn't want us to be hypocrites. He wants us to be able to stand complete before Him (Colossians 2:10). When you think of a person who most completely resembles Christ, what adjectives would you use to describe them?

Does anyone specific come to mind? When I think of a modern-day Christian who is authentic through and through, I think of Billy Graham. He came to be known as "America's pastor."

Born the first of four children, Billy grew up on a dairy farm. He never forgot his humble roots. During his lifetime, he spoke to more than 215 million people in more than 185 countries.

He received the Presidential Medal of Freedom and met with every U.S. president from Harry Truman to Barack Obama. Reverend Graham was listed on the Gallup Annual U.S. Poll of most admired people sixty-one times. That's more than any other world figure!

Why? Because Billy Graham resembled Christ. He spent His life seeking Jesus and leading others to Him. Billy was a man of Godly character. My dad, Clifford Nale, shares much in common with Billy. They're both men of their word.

I've heard it said that your reputation is who people think you are, while your character is who you are...when no one is looking. Billy lived to be ninety-nine years old; both his reputation and his character were always consistent with his faith.

He held himself accountable to Christ, so that his testimony stood the test of time. Did you know that Billy vowed to never be alone in a room with another woman, other than his wife, Ruth? He understood the danger of both temptation and sin.

Regularly, Billy insisted that his crusades be audited and the results be made public to avoid any hint of scandal. He never built a church with his name on it. And he and Ruth raised their family of four children in a modest home in the Blue Ridge Mountains in North Carolina.

Their home was near the farm he grew up on in Charlotte. Billy lived in that home until he was taken to his heavenly home in 2018, when he was nearly 100 years old. Dr. Graham embodied 2 Corinthians 5:20-21 where we learn:

"We are Christ's ambassadors;
God is making his appeal through us.
We speak for Christ when we plead,
'Come back to God!' For God made Christ,

who never sinned, to be the offering for our sin,
so that we could be made right with God through Christ."

People could see that Billy was Christ's ambassador. Though he received a star on the Hollywood Walk of Fame in 1989 and was knighted in 2001 on behalf of Queen Elizabeth, that's not what we remember. We remember his unwavering message of salvation and grace.

Billy once said: "God never takes away something from your life without replacing it with something better." He also insisted: "It is the Holy Spirit's job to convict, God's job to judge and my job to love." Hmm. Loving others is something that we each can do.

Couldn't America use a little less partisan judgement and a lot more love for our fellow Americans? Billy spent a lifetime loving Christ and others. As my Dad would say: "Billy Graham was the real deal."

THE JOURNEY FORWARD:

Like Reverend Graham, I want people to see Christ when they see me. I want to live *fully clothed in Christ* (1 Peter 5:5). Which brings me back to the dickey that was lost in the Christmas wrapping frenzy. May I ask, is your life of faith best represented by a faux collar or a full shirt? Might you consider today if you are completely His or just partially committed to Christ?

ALBERT EINSTEIN HAIR

AND BLUEBERRY PANCAKE SYRUP

*N*ormally my husband wakes up super early to see patients at the hospital, but this morning was different. It was Saturday and he had a weekend off call, so we were snoozing. Then the phone rang.

Dave rolled over to take the call only to learn it was his answering service, who had the wrong doctor. Now that we were awake, we tumbled out of bed to tackle our chores.

My husband headed out back and I started stripping sheets. After loading the washer, I went to the kitchen to prep for breakfast. When searching for the blueberry pancake syrup, I reached up to lock the back door to keep it from being opened and pushing me head first into the pantry.

Later the phone rang. I could hear from caller ID that it was my husband's call service…again. Thinking that they were calling the wrong doctor, I moved on to scrubbing the bathroom sink. After I pulled off my rubber gloves, I transferred a load of sheets to the dryer.

When the phone rang a third time, I muttered, "They just won't leave my poor hubby alone."

When the phone rang a fourth time, I was remaking our bed with warm sheets from the dryer, so I picked up the receiver on our nightstand. That's when I heard a man ask: "Are you trying to kill me?"

Startled, I mouthed nothing. Seconds slipped into silence. Then the voice insisted: "Unlock the door, Lisa!" When he said my name, I recognized his voice...It was my husband!

I raced to the door at the far end of the house. Over an hour ago, I had locked it, when I was on my knees searching for the pancake syrup in the pantry right behind the door. If it were opened then, it would have pushed me headlong into the shelves.

When I flung open the door, there was my sweetheart...but he didn't look a thing like my hubby. This man looked more like Albert Einstein...on a bad hair day. Each strand of Dave's hair stood straight up and there were tiny tufts of what looked like toilet tissue clinging crazily to it.

My husband's face was watermelon red...juicy with sweat. As he stumbled inside, he shook his head, asking in dismay, "Why did you lock the door?"

I replied, "Because I was looking for the blueberry pancake syrup!" Now he looked confused trying to link what a locked door had to do with blueberry syrup. As I attempted to connect the two, he signaled me to stop.

He just wanted to cool off in peace. Sprawling out under the fan as best he could in the straight back, kitchen chair he asked, "Will you bring me some water?" Then he shared his side of the story.

He was working on the pool pump, which was located right under the dryer vent. It was a tight space, so he was forced to stand with his head upside down, bent over to see the pipes that were underneath the vent...which explained his hair.

He had called three times on his cell phone (which had the same caller I.D. as his call service) to ask me to please turn off the dryer. When I didn't pick up, he pounded on the back door and then on the back window. Because I was cleaning on the opposite end of our home, I couldn't hear him.

He had nearly finished fixing the pump and was now held hostage in the backyard, surrounded by the six-foot privacy fence. The gate was padlocked and the key was inside. As much as the gate key, he needed his truck keys, so he could head to the lumber yard for one final part. It was approaching 100 degrees.

AFTER HE COOLED DOWN AND LEFT, I WAS LEFT TO REFLECT, AS I fried bacon for breakfast. How often in the midst of trials do we feel like bacon in life's frying pan, asking God: "Are you trying to kill me?" We are hot and hurt. If God loved us, why would He allow *this* to happen? Have you asked yourself *that* question?

Do you ever feel like you should be exempt from trials?

Sometimes I do, even though I can read verses like 1 Peter 4:12-13:

> "When life gets really difficult,
> don't jump to the conclusion that God isn't on the job.
> Instead, be glad that you are in the very thick
> of what Christ experienced.
> This is a spiritual refining process,
> **with glory just around the corner."**

God promises glory can come *after* refining trials, much like a rainbow can come *after* a gloomy rain. God is never too busy to make time for us, though it sometimes feels that way.

It didn't make sense to my husband that I would lock him out. He was desperate. Have you ever felt locked out and desperate? Have you ever been so tired that you didn't even have the strength to find words to pray? At those times we can take comfort from Romans 8:27 knowing:

> "The moment we get tired in the waiting,
> God's Spirit is right alongside helping us along.
> If we don't know how or what to pray, it doesn't matter.
> He does our praying in and for us,
> making prayer out of our wordless sighs, our aching groans."

When my husband couldn't fathom why I didn't answer the phone or the door, he began to wonder if I couldn't hear him or if I had forgotten about him. He questioned my motives, wondering if I had his best interests at heart. If we're honest, haven't we wondered these same things when we call out to God?

Be assured that while God may not remove the trials, He is beside us in the fire, just as He was with Shadrach, Meshach, and Abednego. They were three Jewish men who were thrown into the fiery furnace when they refused to bow down to worship King Nebuchadnezzar (Daniel 3).

Amazingly the king saw a fourth person in the furnace. The fourth person was the King of all Kings! Although not in human form, Christ is with us in our trials (Psalm 23:4).

We often feel alone asking "why?" In my husband's case, he asked, "**Why did you lock the door?**" Sometimes I feel like God has turned His back on me, even though I know this is simply not true.

Suffering can leave us feeling abandoned, but God promises that He will never leave or forsake us (Hebrews 13:5b). God doesn't lock us out accidentally or purposefully, nor does He ignore our cries.

In fact in Revelation 3:20 we learn that we are the ones that need to "unlock the door" and allow Him in. While you and I are never locked out of His presence, He may not remove the trials, because He knows that it may "unlock the door" to blessings in the future (1 Peter 1:6-7).

This brings us to the last question: "Will you bring me water?" My husband truly needed water. God knows we need more than water; we need a Savior so we never thirst again (John 4:14).

When Dave asked for a drink, I didn't just go to the sink filling a glass from the tap. I went to the fridge filling a glass with crushed ice then cold water. I did this three times, until his thirst was quenched, to make sure he knew of my love and concern for his well-being.

THE JOURNEY FORWARD:

On your journey forward today, can you make time today to read about the four flame-retardant men in Daniel 3:17-18? Are you in awe of their courageous response bolded below? Oh how I pray for that kind of faith under fire!

"If we are thrown into the blazing furnace,
the God whom we serve is able to save us...
But even if he doesn't,
we want to make it clear to you,
Your Majesty, that we will never serve your gods
or worship the gold statue you have set up."

And that, my fellow sojourners, is a **Glimmer of Glory** in a gloomy moment that will never go up in flames and will forever be remembered!

SPARKLERS, SMOKE BOMBS & SNAKES

WRONG + WRONG = WE'RE RIGHT

*M*ost days our bird dogs guard our backyard from butterflies and bunny rabbits, but tonight is different. Betsi and Coco are going nuts, barking and running around in circles as firecrackers explode and smoke fills the summer air.

As German Shorthair Pointers, they're bred to hunt. Squirrels may go nuts over nuts, but our dogs go nuts over squirrels. Add two kids and a flurry of fireworks to the mix and chaos has found new explosive heights.

My husband has visited the red, white and blue tent near the highway to buy "fun stuff for the kids." I smile not knowing who enjoys them more, the kids or him. Ah…the glory of the Fourth of July.

I watch my daughter wiggle her little hips and swing her sparkler pom-poms. She cheers: "Firecracker. Firecracker.

Boom. Boom. Boom." And her eyes twinkle illuminated by the light. I clap both for her and for God, Who once again is allowing me to see **Glimmers of Glory**. I see pure sparkling joy in my daughter who is living in the moment.

Fully present.

Completely happy.

Having fun.

I capture a sliver of her joy in a picture for her Nana and Papa. Alyssa is so proud, taking her sparkler twirling to new heights.

As I was mesmerized by the trail of swirling light left by the sparklers, I was reminded of the passage in Matthew 5:15-16. There we are told by Jesus that we are the light of the world. We are to shine like a city skyline at night. He reminds us that no one lights a lamp and then hides it, saying:

> "Instead, a lamp is placed on a stand,
> where it gives light to everyone in the house.
> In the same way, let your good deeds shine out for all to see,
> so that everyone will praise your heavenly Father.

To paraphrase loosely, we are to be like the sparklers that my daughter uses to bring joy chasing away the darkness and cheering people on. Our good deeds are to "sparkle," bringing **Glimmers of Glory** to others.

Unfortunately, I don't always sparkle as I should. In fact, sometimes my actions might more accurately be characterized by a smoke bomb. Just today as I sat in my car behind a poky driver, who was daydreaming after the light turned green, I fumed red. I was running late for an appointment.

The thoughts I have sometimes find words that obscure the light of Christ, much like the colored cloud of a smoke bomb. St. Paul tells us when we became Christians, we became a "new creation." This means that anyone who belongs to Christ has become a new person. Paul explains that daily we need to put off the old things–the old sin (2 Corinthians 5:17).

Our sin nature could be characterized by the charcoal snake my daughter watches grow from a little black disk. In the book of Genesis in the Garden of Eden, evil is characterized by a snake. Much like the charcoal snake disk grows when ignited by the flame, sin grows when ignited by the flesh and left unchecked by the Holy Spirit.

Just as the resulting toy snake is charred and ugly, the result of our sin nature is ugly. The dark spots on the pavement left behind by the snake are similar to the enduring marks that can be left behind by sin.

So how do we "put off our old sin nature"? That's a question that I ask myself daily. And honestly, the answer looks different every day. Some days it involves praying rather than responding in anger to a comment made by my husband.

Other days it includes being ever so *patient* with my *impatient* toddler, who has more questions than I can answer. Still other days it's carving out the time to make that phone call to speak with a friend or family member who may need to hear a word of love and encouragement when I'd rather just crash on the couch. Do you know the feeling?

What do your days look like when you put others first, loving them like Christ loves us? I've heard it said that the shape of the cross represents the love Christ has for us. The vertical beam of the cross represents the vertical love that God had in sending Christ down to the Earth to die for our sins. The horizontal crossbeam represents the horizontal love that He wants us to show those beside and around us here on Earth.

This cross-shaped concept of love is explained by Paul. He says that because God has brought us back to Him through Christ, we are called "to reconcile" others to Christ. We do this by sharing the Good News that He no longer counts people's sins against them. In this way we are Christ's ambassadors. Paul explains in *2 Corinthians 5:21:

> "God put the **wrong** on him
> who never did anything **wrong**,
> so we could be put **right** with God."

Did you notice God's math? Strangely enough in this verse, two wrongs does make *us* right.

> "Wrong+Wrong=We're Right"
> **W + W = WR**

It's God's miraculous math! Only God and Jesus can pull this equation off with the Holy Spirit. We did nothing to deserve this gift of grace. Freedom through Christ is something to be celebrated, just as we celebrate our nation's freedom. His love for us spans every generation...

every race *and*...

every creed. *It crosses*

every border *of*

every nation.

So while fireworks celebrate America's birth every Fourth of July, let good works commemorate your spiritual birth every day.

THE JOURNEY FORWARD:

On today's journey I just have one reflective question for you. Which would most accurately characterize your flesh today: a sparkler, a smoke bomb or a snake?

Whether it's the Fourth of July or the middle of winter, together we can pledge our allegiance and love for God. As we celebrate our country's freedom, I'm reminded to focus on the freedom that I have in Christ. And I'm challenged to be like a sparkler, providing **Glimmers of Glory** for others.

KNOCK KNOCK

"Knock. Knock." My two-year-old is telling me her joke yet again.

"Who's there, Sweetie?" I say and she giggles. We've been caught in this endless loop all morning. Her response will be the same tiring...

"Knock. Knock, Mommy," she repeats.

Again I ask, "Who's there?" I try to explain that she is supposed to say "Howl."

Then I would ask "Howl who?"

Then she would respond: "Howl you gonna know unless you open the door?"

My efforts are fruitless, as she thinks her version of the joke is much funnier. She doesn't understand the concept of a punch line.

"Knock. Knock." She tugs on my shorts as she furrows her brow and insists: "Ask 'whods dare?'"

"Who's there, Precious?" She knocks on my leg and begins the joke again. If only we had the same enthusiasm and persistence of my daughter when we "knock" in prayer on the pearly gates!

JESUS TEACHES US HOW TO PRAY GIVING US THE "THE LORD'S Prayer" (Luke 11). Then immediately following, He tells a story about two friends. He asks us to imagine what would happen if you went to a friend's house in the middle of the night asking for bread. He explains that visitors showed up at your home unannounced and you have no food on hand.

Your friend responds saying he has just gotten the kids to bed and locked the door. He's tucked in for the night and asks that you please stop bothering him as he's exhausted.

Then Jesus shares that even if your neighbor won't get up because he's your friend, you need to stand your ground. He encourages you to keep knocking. And He says that He will finally answer, providing whatever you need.

Christ concludes this parable in *Luke 11:10 with these promises:

> "Ask and you'll get;
> Seek and you'll find;
> Knock and the door will open."

While this exact scenario may seem unlikely given that we have convenience stores in America that are open all night, what He shares concerning prayer is meant for all people... in every nation...spanning every generation.

The Friend and Neighbor represents our Heavenly Father. Having taught us **what** to pray with "The Lord's Prayer," Jesus uses this story to teach us **when** to pray. He tells us to pray whenever we have a need, even if it's the middle of the night.

Now I have many friends–even several close friends–but none have appeared on my front porch at midnight groveling for groceries. Jesus uses hyperbole to make a point. The message is that we can and should bring our needs to our Father **anytime**.

He's more than a neighbor and more than a friend. He's our Father. This puts the whole story in a new light. Even though none of my friends have begged for bread at bedtime, my daughter wakes me up most nights.

She comes our room, tugs on the covers and implores, "Thirsty Mama." If she happens to be hungry too she tells me so. And plain bread won't do. She asks for her favorite "pantakes."

In this parable, Jesus shows us that the same relationship exists between God and His children. The focus of this story is to teach us **how** to pray. Jesus tells us to be confident and persistent, emboldening us to keep "asking," "seeking" and "knocking."

Did you notice the increasing intensity? Anyone can *ask*, but not everyone *seeks*, which implies persistence. Finally, when we *knock* we have to physically engage.

This requires grit. On this journey to find God moments, persistence and engagement is key.

So may I ask you, when you knock on someone's door, how many times do you knock before you walk away? What's customary? I may knock in two sets of three, but then I quit, not wanting to be intrusive.

In this technological age, knocking is similar to texting. How many times do you text someone before you quit reaching out? Please know that God has given you permission to keep reaching out again and again. He encourages it!

Can you think of one long-standing prayer for which you have petitioned God? Have you stopped knocking and merely substituted with tapping? Honestly, sometimes I have.

I've known others who don't knock because they've grown accustomed to being autonomous. We're not expected to be self-sufficient, just as a child is not self-sufficient. We are God's children.

Can you and I learn persistence from those, like my daughter, who readily knock…even when their need is just to be heard telling jokes? I know I can.

After teaching us what, when and how to pray, Jesus concludes, asking in Luke 11:11-13:

> "If your little boy asks for a serving of fish,
> do you scare him with a live snake on his plate?
> If your little girl asks for an egg,
> do you trick her with a spider?"

Then Jesus acknowledges that as imperfect as we are, we wouldn't purposefully hurt our children. And He reassures us, sharing:

> "How much more will your heavenly Father
> give the Holy Spirit to those who ask him?"

I find His last statement very telling. He will give His Spirit "to those who *ask*." We have *to ask*. Yes, God knows what we need. But we're told we still need to come to Him and *ask*.

He teaches us how to pray with "The Lord's Prayer." But He gives us more than a prayer when He tells the story of the friend who comes to borrow bread. And then He tells us about a father giving good gifts to his hungry children.

Jesus **motivates** us to pray when He tells us how ready our Father is to answer our prayers! It seems that He's just waiting for us to ask.

Yet there are times when we knock as long and as hard as we know how, and it seems that God doesn't answer our prayers. I don't understand why God answers some prayers and others He doesn't.

Sometimes my daughter may not understand why I grant some of her requests, but others I don't. And she never likes it when my response is delayed. She may want dessert, but the answer may be "no," until she has eaten her healthy food.

Often she doesn't understand my reasoning. But someday I hope she will. Likewise, we may not understand God's reasoning, but I think we will better understand from heaven's perspective.

Which brings me back to my sweet daughter, who didn't understand the punch line to the joke she was telling. What she had mastered in that moment was persistence. Her persistence was rooted in her desire for my attention because she knows that I love and value her.

Please know that God loves and values you dearly as His child (1 John 3:1).

THE JOURNEY FORWARD:

Be motivated to knock on God's door in prayer, knowing that He will never forget you as He promises in Isaiah 49:15-16:

> "Can a mother forget the infant at her breast,
> walk away from the baby she bore?
> But even if mothers forget,
> I'd never forget you—never.
> Look, I've written your names on the backs of my hands."

DADDY FIX IT

$\mathcal{W}$hen I was a little girl, my Dad could fix anything! He fixed my Barbie's® knee that was torqued awkwardly forward, my baby's decapitated head, and my stuck playhouse windows. You name it; he knew how to make it better.

My Daddy was BIG and I was his precious little one. I was convinced there was nothing he couldn't do. Not knowing the first of the Ten Commandments, I idolized my Daddy. He was the best.

Today I see my three-year-old daughter following in my footsteps. My husband and Alyssa are close and love each others' company. If something in the house won't work, she offers: "I'll take it to **my** Daddy. Daddy fix it."

She has no hesitancy and no doubts. He greets her with open arms, stops whatever he's doing, meets her need, and makes her little corner of the world glimmer again. She relishes time spent with her Daddy.

When she eats dinner from his plate on his lap, she eats better than she does at any other time of the day. And if Daddy is eating broccoli, she eats broccoli...and likes it! Hominy, okra, squash, salad with blue cheese dressing...you name it, she'll eat it and ask for more, if her Daddy does. It seems she would eat dryer lint if he did.

It doesn't matter what he's doing; if he likes it, she likes it. Take football, for example. I always thought my daughter, like myself, would have no interest in it, but she loves it. Either something is "icky" or "happy." I am baffled to say she insists, "Football happy, Momma."

No matter how "icky" the situation, our Heavenly Father, or Abba, can help heal broken hearts and broken lives. He promises in Romans 8:28 that:

> "all things work together for good
> to those who love God,
> to those who are the called according to His purpose."

While God reassures us that every detail in our lives can be worked **into** something good, He did not say that every detail **is** good. Brokenness due to abuse is *not* good. Sickness is *not* good. Violence is *not* good.

Can you think of other examples of things in life that are *not* good? But God promises us believers that He can and will use even those things that are "not good" to "bring good."

In your life has God ever brought good out of a circumstance that was "not good"? If so, your life stands as a testimony to others on their journey. Have you shared your witness?

If you're in the middle of a trial that is "not good," it's easy to become discouraged. We can have moments of doubt. But doubt and doom have no right to dominate, for Paul reminds us that if God is for us, no one will prevail against us (Romans 8:31).

When our will is aligned with God's will and we call on Christ there's no challenge that can crush us who believe. We're told that we will face challenges and sorrows in this life, but we're to be encouraged because He has defeated the world (John 16:33).

The Bible is clear that being Christian doesn't exempt us from hardships. But we're inspired to be lighthearted because He has everything under control.

There's no situation that the Spirit cannot improve. St. Paul reminds us that God didn't hesitate to come to our rescue, embracing us when we were at our worst. He sent His Own Son, which is His greatest expression of love. Knowing that there isn't anything He wouldn't do for us, no one can come up against us and win. In *Romans 8:34 we learn:

"The One who died for us
—who was raised to life for us!—

is in the presence of God at this very moment sticking up for us."

Does it amaze you to think that Jesus is in God's presence "sticking up for us"? He continues on in verse 35-39 asking if we think that anyone is going to be able to "drive a wedge" between us and God's love. Paul says that's not going to happen and then shares:

> "Not trouble, not hard times, not hatred, not hunger,
> not homelessness, not bullying threats, not backstabbing,
> not even the worst sins listed in Scripture
> will separate us from Christ's love."

God will never stop loving us. No matter what sin we may commit or failures we experience, we are His children. Likewise, my husband will never stop loving our daughter, no matter what she does or fails to do.

As his child she's given special privileges. Only she can sit on his lap at dinner and have the first choice of everything on his plate. My husband invests in our daughter. As a result, she has learned that her Daddy is trustworthy. Even something that stinks as bad as blue cheese, she accepts from his hand.

She comes running when he walks through the door and squeals in excitement. She loves to hear his voice when he calls her name. This is an image that holds a deeper truth. Like Alyssa, at three, who trusts her father, should we trust our Heavenly Father? I believe so.

In fact, when His disciples thought He was too exhausted to deal with children, Jesus corrected them saying they were to let the children come to Him because the Kingdom of Heaven belongs to them (Matthew 19:14). Then Jesus placed His hands on their head and blessed them.

Just as my husband makes time for Alyssa, I know that our Abba sees the eternal picture and can work even the rotten-smelling "Roquefort" things into good.

While our lives are broken and marred with imperfection, nothing is beyond God's ability to save. Jesus was a carpenter–a Master of mending. His Father knows how to fix both wooden parts and broken hearts, making them better than new.

I want to trust my Heavenly Father, as my daughter trusts her earthly father. Okra and summer squash, like some trials, may not initially *seem good*, but can God work them together *for good*? That's the promise of Romans 8:28.

I'll be honest, it's the senseless suffering and the pointless violence that I struggle with most, even in light of this Scripture. I think Jesus understood that there will be many things beyond our comprehension. Things too big and too bad for even those with the highest degrees in the holiest of studies.

Which is why He chooses to tell us to be like "little children" who were drawn to Him, who crawled up on His lap. He was torn and tired, but He was never too tired for a child. And He is never too tired for us–His children.

THE JOURNEY FORWARD:

My daughter proclaims with no hesitancy, "My Daddy fix it!" Though she uses the wrong verb tense, we hear her faith message clearly.

How long has it been since you have taken a problem to your heavenly Father? Is there a gloomy memory or circumstance you can take to Him right now, asking Him to replace it with a **Glimmer of Glory**? The more we rely on Him, the more our children and those we love will learn to rely on Him by our example.

HARLOT IN THE HALL OF FAME

*H*ave you ever felt like you're not worthy to be used by God? I have. And have you thought that He should use someone else to accomplish His mission? Me too. Sometimes do you wonder how He could use you to make a difference? I do.

Although a part of you wants to please God, another part of you feels like it isn't possible. If you're like me, somedays you're working just to keep your head above water. How could God possibly use us to save others who are drowning in hopelessness?

I suspect like me, you don't feel strong enough or "holy" enough to be involved in God's work. Secretly, you feel inadequate when it comes to spiritual matters.

There are so many people who know more...who do

more...who seem to lead a better life. They're the kind of people that God calls. Right?

GOD WELCOMES AND CAN USE ANYONE WHO HAS A WILLING HEART. He plays no favorites. We all are on a journey, and He can use us right where we are, just as He used a woman named Rahab.

In the great walled city of Jericho well over 1,000 years before Christ came, God looked at the heart of Rahab. He didn't look at her profession nor did He look at her religion, or lack thereof. He looked at her willingness to stand in the gap...her willingness to come when called. She happened to earn a living as a prostitute.

In the first chapter of Joshua, we can read about her story. She offered refuge to the two spies that Joshua–the leader of the troops of the Hebrew nation–had sent into the city of Jericho.

You may remember her story. She covered the spies with the stalks of flax on her rooftop. When the soldiers of Jericho came looking for the spies, she told them that they had left the city.

Why did she betray her king and people? We learn that they were afraid of the Israelites, knowing defeat was likely. They had heard how God had parted the Red Sea for the Hebrew nation when they fled from Egypt years earlier (Joshua 2).

Her people remembered how the Hebrews had defeated the two Amorite Kings–Og and Sihon–completely destroying their people. Then Rahab shares in verse 11:

"'No wonder our hearts have melted in fear!
No one has the courage to fight after hearing such things. For
the Lord your God is the supreme
God of the heavens above and the earth below.'"

Rahab believed in God. She knew by the power of His works providing for His people that He was God of the heavens and of the earth. She wanted to be on God's side, saving herself and her family.

The defeat of Jericho was key, and Rahab was key to that defeat. The victory was strategically important. It encouraged the Hebrew people, as they began their quest to conquer the Holy Land.

If the Lord can use Rahab, then He can use you and me. Wouldn't you agree? Yet there's more to the story of this lady and her simple faith. Not only do we read about her in the book of Joshua, but we find Rahab again, not once, not twice, but three times in the New Testament and in the most unlikely of places.

First, we read about her in the opening lines of the New Testament, when St. Matthew names the honored lineage of Christ. In Matthew 1:5 we read that she became part of the family of King David and ultimately of Christ. Her prior profession did not exclude her from the most important genealogy known to man.

Secondly, we find Rahab in Hebrews 11–the great faith chapter. Shes listed in the Bible's "Hall of Fame for Faith" along with such great patriarchs as Noah, Abraham, Isaac, Jacob,

Moses, and King David. She and Sarah, the matriarch of our faith, are the only two women among these famous men. I'm sure she never thought that was possible.

Finally we can read that her faith was evident by her **willingness to help**. She's compared to Abraham, establishing the link between her faith and works in Hebrews 11:31:

> "Rahab could have lost her life for hiding the spies.
> She could have brought destruction on her entire household,
> but because she knew that God would help the Hebrew nation,
> she too wanted to help them."

She wanted to help. Though the stakes were high, she stands as an example...as someone willing to be used by God. That willingness–that step in faith–pleased God then, and pleases Him now.

In fact we read in *Hebrews 11:6:

> "It's impossible to please God apart from faith.
> And why?
> Because anyone who wants to approach God
> must believe both that he exists and that he cares
> enough to respond to those who seek him."

Rahab was rewarded for her faith. We all will be. If you're a believer, no matter how imperfect you may feel, you're called by God.

Why? Because as a believer, you not only bear the name of

Christ, you have Him living in your heart. Through Him you are made holy. By Him you are commissioned (Matthew 28:18-20).

THE JOURNEY FORWARD:

On our journey forward, God is with us through the good and the gloomy. The calm and the chaotic. Our faithfulness and our failures. Whatever your profession, God can use you right where you're at. While you most likely won't be asked to hide spies, can you look for someone today that might be hiding behind a harsh exterior or a forced smile that desperately needs your help? He can use you, as He used Rahab, to bring **Glimmers of Glory**.

BABY JESUS AND HUMPTY DUMPTY

*M*y daughter was born three days after baby Jesus...three days and 1,992 years after Him. And ironically on her second Christmas, she broke baby Jesus. Almost two and barely tall enough to stretch her pudgy little hand up into the nativity manger, she kidnapped the tiny ceramic baby.

He was perfect...just the right size. She knew she was only supposed to look at the baby but not touch the baby. So it was doubly thrilling to have Jesus in her hands. As any wannabe momma would, Alyssa wanted to rock her baby. So she pushed her tiny rocking chair from her carpeted bedroom to the tiled kitchen.

It was a special rocking chair with a music box on the bottom curved band that played precious lullabies when fueled by movement. She was smart and knew that the chair had to be on a hard surface for the music box to be activated.

Before she sat down, she needed a tiny blanket to swaddle baby Jesus. A dish cloth would be perfect and she knew just where to find one. She felt so BIG! As she rocked, the lullaby played. Then the unthinkable happened.

Alyssa dropped baby Jesus.

His head broke off.

She cried.

I cried.

Why couldn't she have broken a leg off a sheep or a tail off a cow? But baby Jesus...He was the focus of the entire Nativity set.

This was the one Christmas decoration for which I had splurged. It was handmade by an older couple from church and was the first exquisite Christmas decoration I bought after becoming a pharmacist.

Every year it is the first decoration I set up and the last decoration I take down. It is displayed in the highest place of honor, right inside our front door for everyone to see. I treasured it. But as I looked into her teary eyes, I knew. She was sorry. She wanted me to make it better.

Whether she sobbed because her baby was broken or because she knew she was in trouble, it was impossible to know. I didn't know whether I was more frustrated with her for disobeying or with myself for having placed something I treasured within her reach.

Unlike Humpty Dumpty though, it didn't take all the king's

horses and all the king's men–just me and Mr. Elmer–to put baby Jesus back together again.

Years from now, the memories that I'll have when I gaze at that tiny figure will be priceless. Our Jesus has been personalized by my daughter's hands.

AFTER THE ACCIDENT, I WAS LEFT TO REFLECT. JUST AS ALYSSA'S disobedience led to Jesus being broken, my disobedience led to Jesus being broken…through His death on the cross.

How often do I "lose my head and come unglued," when it comes to the little things in life? A gouge in the woodwork, juice on the carpet or ketchup in the car seat. You know, the incidental accidents.

These are the little frustrations that plague our days as moms. They're definitely not things that we should lose our heads over, I tell myself. At times when I'm upset, I remind myself that life is short and turn to the short verse found in Psalm 90:12:

> "Teach us to realize the brevity of life
> so that we may grow in wisdom."

This is one sentence with fifteen words that I can repeat as I'm cleaning up something that's broken or spilled. It calms my frustration and helps me see life from an eternal perspective.

Jesus always kept things in perspective, even when He was

being pressured by the haughty Pharisees. He didn't crack under pressure, like I might have.

In Mark 2:23-28 we learn about the time when Jesus and His disciples were walking through some grain fields on the Sabbath. Because they were hungry, they picked the ripened grain to eat. Since the religious leaders were looking to find fault with Jesus and His ministry, they immediately jumped at the opportunity to "come unglued" and "lose their heads." They wanted to make the point that Jesus broke the law. Gasp!

But Jesus understood the reason for the Sabbath. He reminded them that King David went to the house of God when he was starving and in need (1 Samuel 21:6). While David broke the law by eating the sacrificial loaves of bread meant for the priests, Jesus explained that God understands our needs. He clarified in Mark 2:27:

"The Sabbath was made to meet the needs of people,
and not people to meet the requirements of the Sabbath."

If Jesus were in my kitchen watching my sweet Alyssa swaddle a ceramic figure of Him, I'm sure He would have been touched by her kindness. He came to Earth to be a living sacrifice broken *for* her. To have the ceramic figurine of Him quite literally broken *by* her is a reminder of the price He paid out of love.

In Colossians 3:1-2 we're reminded of Jesus' sacrifice:

"Since you have been raised to new life with Christ,

set your sights on the realities of heaven,
where Christ sits in the place of honor at God's right hand.
Think about the things of heaven, not the things of earth."

When our days are filled with broken dreams, broken health and broken hearts, He encourages us to think about the "things of heaven, not the things of earth."

On earth, there will always be brokenness. In heaven, brokenness will be healed, not just glued back together with a bottle of Elmer's.

I'm pretty good at patching things up with paste then touching them up with paint, but I have a long way to go relaxing with Jesus in the reality of *Matthew 6:32-33:

"What I'm trying to do here is to get you to relax,
to not be so preoccupied with *getting*,
so you can respond to God's *giving*.
People who don't know God and the way he works
fuss over these things, but you know both God
and how he works.
Steep your life in God-reality,
God-initiative, God-provisions."

Do you sometimes need to "relax" and not "fuss," losing your head over the small things? Like me, do you need to "steep your life in God-reality" much like you would steep your tea bag in a cup of hot water? I admit that I need to infuse my mind daily with God's promises. Then I can see **Glimmers of Glory** even in the gloomy, broken moments when my life–like the ceramic baby Jesus–seems to be in pieces.

THE JOURNEY FORWARD:

On your journey forward, do you have a delicate tea cup and saucer that you can use as you purposefully carve out time to spend relaxing in His presence, infusing yourself with this promise from Philippians 4:6-7:

"Don't worry about anything; instead, pray about everything.
Tell God what you need, and thank him for all he has done.
Then you will experience God's peace,
which exceeds anything we can understand.
His peace will guard your hearts and minds
as you live in Christ Jesus."

During my quiet times, I have found that Jesus Christ calms me even more than a cup of Earl Grey. I'm reminded that He didn't lose His head and come unglued when those around Him cracked under pressure. He can help us keep it together too.

ENEMIES

*A*s I stood in line this morning, I saw an unlikely trio of faces posted on the wall before me. There was Marilyn Monroe and Elvis Presley with Martin Luther King Jr. sandwiched between them.

I smiled back at the trio. Below them were several styles of stars and stripes. The U.S. Postal Service aims to please when offering their choice of stamps.

Now that it's Christmas, there are even more choices. The decision can be tough and time consuming. Take it from a bedraggled mom with a couple of cranky kiddos. We stood behind a sweet but indecisive lady at the post office today during the Saturday morning rush.

I'm efficient and always choose the same design. Hands down, my favorite are the love stamps. Now there are two styles of those. Good golly...life is more complex with choices.

I remember when stamps didn't come with adhesive and I had to lick the back for Christmas cards. While licking I had time to reflect on how much a "roll" of love stamps had in common with our "role" of loving our enemies.

STAMPS SEEM TO COST A LOT. LIKEWISE, LOVING OUR ENEMIES **costs** a lot. We put aside the **wealth** of anger we feel and **invest** in forgiveness.

We **spend** time to express that love. We **foreclose** on any resentment. We **subtract** harsh words. We look beyond the person's **debt** of wrongs.

We **credit** them as one of God's children. And finally we **count** our blessings. It **costs** us plenty...much more than **pocket change** to **change** our attitudes.

When we mail a letter to someone it **costs** us, not the recipient. We **pay** the price of the stamp. As Christians, it costs us, as we are called to **pay** (or repay) evil with good.

In Matthew 5:45 Jesus tells us to love our enemies and pray for those who persecute us, saying:

> "In that way, you will be acting as
> true children of your Father in heaven.
> For he gives his sunlight to both the evil and the good,
> and he sends rain on the just and the unjust alike."

This is an easy verse to read, but it is hard to live. Doesn't it seem unfair that bad people get good gifts too? There's a part of me that wants them to live without light and wither without rain, because that's what they deserve.

But Jesus isn't about giving people what they deserve. He is about grace when He asks in verse 46:

> "If you love only those who love you,
>   what reward is there for that?
> Even corrupt tax collectors do that much."

Experience tells me that loving our enemies can get sticky... much stickier than the back side of a stamp. Our enemies may wonder about our ulterior motive. How could we possibly compliment them?

What could we mean when we ask how they are doing? Why should we or how could we care? Ultimately, much like the glue that sticks the stamp to the envelope, our love sticks to them.

Love transforms (2 Corinthians 5:17). Even though the result may not be instantaneous or even outwardly apparent, love brings change. Stamps too have changed a lot over the years.

Now the USPS has introduced Forever Stamps that you can purchase at the current price, and when rates rise the stamp is still valid. With ever-increasing postage costs, Forever Stamps are great as they last forever.

I see similarities between Forever Stamps and the love described in 1 Corinthians 13:13. There we learn:

"Three things will last **forever**
—faith, hope, and love—
and the greatest of these is love.

Loving those who are unkind doesn't sound pleasant. For those of us who remember licking the back of stamps: Was it pleasant? Now for the stickier question: Was it needed?

There have been times when my stamp didn't stay stuck to the envelope or times I've forgotten to attach a stamp before mailing a letter. Every time it was returned.

Likewise, every time Jesus was asked what was most important, He returns to His message to love others. In fact He summarized all 613 Mitzvot (or commands) of the Old Testament, telling us to love God and love others as you would love yourself (Matthew 22:37-40). Sometimes we make living our faith more difficult than it needs to be.

L–O–V–E. Four letters spell one word. Marilyn Monroe, Elvis Presley and Martin Luther King Jr. were three very different people with very different life goals. Though each had different professions and different backgrounds, they had more in common than living in 1960 and being featured on a stamp.

They each needed love. You and I need love. So in the end, we aren't so different from Marilyn, Elvis and Martin.

THE JOURNEY FORWARD:

Can you think of someone unfriendly, perhaps someone you

would call an enemy? Can you think of one way today that you could express love toward them? Why not mail them a nice note...perhaps with a love stamp?

GLITTER NAIL POLISH

My big sister loved Camp Na-Wa-Kwa. Every year I thought I would too…until I spent one night with daddy longlegs surrounding my bed, instead of my Daddy to tuck me in bed. I just wasn't brave…and I cried.

It wouldn't matter how many weeks I had spent in anticipation, buying calamine lotion, candy and camping gear. I remember tediously painting a wooden fruit crate red, white and blue one year for a nightstand. Even then, I was an interior decorator.

When Kathy was old enough, she became a camp counselor. I was proud to be her little sister. She would sit at my table in the lodge at mealtime. Her presence would comfort me. When I would leave with my Girl Scout troop, she would slip me a little something. I still remember the bottle of glitter nail polish that she slid in my pocket.

By the end of the week, I was covered with mosquito bites and wanted desperately to go home; I whimpered silently at night. Nail polish clutched in one hand and flashlight in the other, I remember pulling the sleeping bag over my head to shut out the bugs and the darkness.

But try as I might, I couldn't shut out the homesickness that settled in my upset tummy. Even though my tent was full of giggling Girl Scouts, I missed my family.

Camp was scary. There were snakes and spiders. There were outdoor latrines that stunk. There was slime in the pond. I wanted to feel safe and have my Mom and Dad under a real roof.

Somehow knowing that my big sister was somewhere in the camp comforted me, when my parents were a whole state away. Just having a familiar face...someone who recognized me...someone to be excited to see me...that made the seven days at camp more bearable.

Now you may not have a week of Camp Na-Wa-Kwa in your summer schedule, but can't a week of work be as fear-filled as a forest? While you may not have to go canoeing upstream, as a Christian there are times you are called to paddle upstream against the cultural current.

Even if you don't have to fight off mosquitoes, there are times when friends seem more like foes that bite. And while there's nothing quite like the odor of outdoor latrines, don't some of the policies, attitudes and responsibilities at work stink?

So even though you don't have to force down cold Beanie-Weenies, there are still tough times that are hard to swallow. During those stints, I find comfort in God's response to the suffering writer of Psalm 40:2:

> "He lifted me out of the pit of despair,
>   out of the mud and the mire.
> He set my feet on solid ground
>   and steadied me as I walked along."

At Girl Scout camp I still recall "the mud and the mire" in the swimming pond next to the main lodge. I cringe remembering how slimy the ladder on the dock felt and how my feet would sink into the mud that squished between my toes.

Summers in Illinois are hot and humid, so I was grateful for a place to swim. But at the same time, I was grossed out by all the green goo. I longed for my own backyard and the little swimming pool my Dad had made that had clean, chlorinated water. I missed everything about home.

My big sister was my "comforter at camp." Now that I'm an adult and know Christ, I have another Comforter. In John 14:16,18, Jesus tells us that He must leave.

He also explains that He will talk to His Father, Who will provide us with the Holy Spirit so we will never be alone. Then He describes the Holy Spirit as our Friend and our Comforter.

As Christians, we each have the Holy Spirit with us, no matter where we find ourselves. This is reassuring.

In times of difficulties and trials, a physical body to offer a big hug sure helps us feel more loved. Together we form the body of Christ. While we have become used to hearing this phrase, it serves a very practical purpose.

We represent Christ here on Earth. Because He is not physically here to reach out to people who are lonely and need reassured, we are called to act on His behalf. If you have ever been on the receiving end of Christ's love, you have experienced His goodness.

We are told to be there for others to be brothers and sisters in Christ. God's greatest commandment–as recapped by Christ–is to love the Lord your God and love others (Mark 12:30-31).

THE JOURNEY FORWARD:

As Christians, how are we helping those around us who are lonely? While a bottle of glitter nail polish may not cheer them up, we can offer a hug, a smile or a heartfelt compliment.

If you are battling loneliness, might you make it your reflex to reach out to someone with kindness? You don't need any glittery words. Just a plain, "I care about you and want to help," could provide them with warming **Glimmers of Glory**.

LET THERE BE LIGHT

*A*t four in the morning, my husband and I were fast asleep. We didn't hear my daughter tiptoe from her bed across the hall to our room. With the delicate chair from her tea table, she climbed up to reach the light switch and…voilà! She gave new meaning to Genesis 1:3:

> "Let there be light:
> and there was L-I-G-H-T!"

My husband bolted upright and, after seeing Alyssa, plopped back down pulling the pillow over his head with a sigh. As I flopped my feet to the floor, my precocious daughter hurried me, saying: "Hungry Mommy. Eat!" She had her hands on her hips for added emphasis. Having just discovered how to use light switches, she devoured the power over light and darkness with a jubilant plea, shouting: "I need pantakes Momma."

HOW MANY PEOPLE THAT WE KNOW ARE HUNGRY FOR THE LIGHT of all lights, Jesus Christ? They may not identify their emptiness as a craving for their Creator. They may feel battered and drained, craving rest and peace. Loneliness may linger. Depression may entomb them.

As we journey together searching for **Glimmers of Glory**, do we notice those around us who may not know how satisfying the Bread of Life can be, never having been filled by Him? Jesus Himself offers us the invitation to come to Him when we are weary and need rest, telling us in Matthew 11:29 to:

> "Take my yoke upon you.
> Let me teach you,
> because I am humble and gentle at heart,
> and you will find rest for your souls."

Today I need rest for my soul. Even though it's early in the morning, I am already weary not having gotten a full night's rest. This verse brings me comfort.

Though Jesus does not promise that there will be no storms, He does promise that we will be given *rest*. And when we are pulling life's load, we will share the yoke with Him. This yoke refers to the wooden neck piece shared by oxen. An experienced ox would typically be paired with a young ox that was quite literally "learning the ropes."

I personally can't think of anyone with whom I would rather work side by side, step by step. Don't you know that Jesus would definitely do His fair share of the work...plus some. In fact He tells us that the burden will be light when we are yoked with Him.

THE JOURNEY FORWARD:

Next time you find yourself awake in the wee hours of the morning, whether by a hungry toddler or more likely by a wearisome worry, tiptoe from your bedroom and switch on the light to read Luke 11:34:

> "Your eye is a lamp, lighting up your whole body.
> If you live wide-eyed in wonder and belief,
> your body fills up with light."

LAWNS AND LIVES

*W*hich requires more effort: housework or lawn work? The answer you're given at the Wilt residence depends on who you ask: my husband or me. One thing we agree upon is that both demand dedication.

Since it's spring, we have focused our efforts on the lawn. It is amazing how May rolls out her red carpet for the green grass. She has also ushered in some unwanted visitors.

The crabgrass and dandelions were not invited, and the grass we hoped would R.S.V.P. to fill in the bare spots near the curb must have misplaced their invitations. The perennials have a standing invitation, but several this year opted not to make an appearance. Meanwhile, our shrubs are like old guests that need to be groomed.

HAVE YOU EVER STOPPED TO THINK HOW MUCH OUR LAWNS HAVE in common with our lives? Lush lawns require a gardener. Fruitful lives require a Master Gardener too. *Galatians 5:22-23 is like *Gardening 101,* as we learn that when we live God's way, He:

"Brings gifts into our lives,
much the same way that fruit appears in an orchard—
things like affection for others,
exuberance about life, serenity.

We develop a willingness to stick with things,
a sense of compassion in the heart and
a conviction that a basic holiness permeates things and people.

We find ourselves involved in loyal commitments,
not needing to force our way in life,
able to marshal and direct our energies wisely."

When we become Christians, we are given His Spirit and Christ makes His home in our hearts. Then we have a decision to make, much like after we purchase a home. We can choose to clear away the weeds and brush of business then plant seeds of good deeds. We can purposefully spend time soaking in the Light of the Son to "ripen" the fruit of the Spirit. Similarly, we can choose to landscape the lawn. Both require dedication; both can be seen by our neighbors.

Our lives stand as a testimony to our dedication to Christ,

just as our lawns stand as a testimony to our dedication to home ownership. A yard can be beautifully landscaped or it can be ignored and become overgrown with unruly weeds. The choice is ours.

THE JOURNEY FORWARD:

My heart's lawn has a few patches of crabgrass that need some work. I have gloomy moments when I am crabby with my family.

On your journey forward today, what areas of your life need that touch of a Master Gardener? The written word is powerful. Can you write in the space below what needs God's "Weed-B-Gon"?

FEAR FACEDOWN

AND THE WAR OF THE NEURONS

I shriek in horror as I see my precious daughter floating facedown in our backyard pool. Every night since we opened the pool several weeks ago I have the same nightmare and now I've woken my tired husband up again.

I'm sorry. I'm sweating. And I'm sitting straight up. Drowning in darkness. Telling myself repeatedly, it was only a dream. Only. A. Dream.

Slipping out of bed, across the hallway and into my daughter's bedroom, I see that she is peacefully sucking her thumb. Her pointer finger is resting beside her pudgy little nose. For the second time tonight, I check to make sure the back door is bolted and the alarm set. I reassure myself that there is no way Alyssa could wander out to the pool and drown. But the image of her floating facedown haunts me.

How many nights will I wake up drenched in the fear of her

drowning? A picture says a thousand words, and I have prayed one thousand prayers for her safety. Have you ever experienced similar dreams that involve your loved one's well-being? Does worry ever steal your sleep?

I have all the telltale signs of panic attacks. As a pharmacist, I understand the physiology of these attacks. I am a sleepless hostage in the raging "War of the Neurons."

In my cortex—the portion of my brain responsible for higher reasoning—my neurons are heroically sharing the news that there is nothing to fear. Unfortunately, they are losing the battle to the mighty neurons hidden deep within the limbic area of my brain that are responsible for my emotions.

Fear—like a stealth bomber—slipped into my otherwise peaceful dreams unnoticed, then dropped its fury of fear. Nothing disturbs me more than dreams which bring disaster to my children. What causes you to fear? Does fear ever bully you at night?

Rather than remain a prisoner of fear, I turn on a light. Then I turn to the Light, opening my Bible to a story I had long forgotten about a man named Gideon. I can relate to Gideon because he too struggled with fear. In Judges 6 we read that he lived at a time when the Israelites were being "reduced to starvation by the Midianites."

In verse 13, Gideon asks questions, that I have asked:

"If the Lord is with us, why has all this happened to us?
And where are all the miracles our ancestors told us about?"

Have you ever felt abandoned and asked similar questions?
Gideon and his fellow countrymen were oppressed by the Midianites, as his ancestors were once oppressed by the Egyptians,
when they were enslaved for 400 years. Gideon wanted answers,
but he didn't want the answer he got in Judges 6:14:

> "Then the Lord turned to him and said,
> 'Go with the strength you have,
> and rescue Israel from the Midianites.
> **I am sending you!**'"

Yikes! Not what he expected. Gideon quickly pointed out
that he was not qualified, because his family was the least
powerful among his people. For good measure, he added that he
was the weakest in his entire family. But the Lord promised to
be with him and to help him destroy the Midianite people, as if
they were a single person.

The angel of the Lord saw something in Gideon that he
didn't see in himself and addresses Gideon as a "mighty hero."
Did you know that Gideon is the only person in the Bible that is
ever addressed as a mighty hero?

The King James Bible calls him a "man of mighty valor," and
The Message Bible simply gives him the title of "mighty warrior." I
find this intriguing that God saw beyond Gideon's excuses and
fear.

Reading further, in verse 34 we learn that the Spirit of the Lord "clothed Gideon with power." I remember feeling "clothed with power" when I bought a power suit for my first job interview after graduation. Coupled with prayer, I felt prepared and strong. What do you do when you need a confidence boost?

Gideon asked for several signs to confirm that it was truly the Lord's Will that he lead an army against the Midianites. He also amassed the largest possible army. Then we read in Judges 7:2-3 that Gideon had too many warriors to fight the enemy. The Lord said:

> "If I let all of you fight the Midianites,
> the Israelites will boast to me that
> they saved themselves by their own strength."

So God asked Gideon to let anyone who was afraid go home. We read that 22,000 were glad to be given an escape clause, leaving only 10,000 who were willing to fight.

Then something even more astonishing happens in verses 4-6. The Lord told Gideon that there were still too many warriors. So He asked that Gideon bring them down to the spring to drink, dividing the warriors into two groups.

In the first group, Gideon gathered all those men who lapped with their tongues, the way dogs lap; in the second group, Gideon gathered those who knelt down and drank from their cupped hands.

Only 300 men drank from their cupped hands. The Lord told Gideon in verse 7:

"With these 300 men I will rescue you and
give you victory over the Midianites.
Send all the others home."

Gideon would face thousands of Midianites, their mortal enemy, with just 300 men. Yikes!

By this point in the story, the image of my daughter floating facedown had vanished. I was caught up in the excitement of the impending battle.

The Lord told Gideon that He had given them victory. But God saw that Gideon was still fearful and needed reassurance. So the Lord directed him to go with his trusty servant into the enemy's camp to listen to what they were saying.

Gideon headed down to the edge of the enemy camp. Like a swarm of locusts, the vast armies of Midian, Amalek and the people of the east had camped in the valley. Their camels were as numerous as grains of sand on the beach.

Gideon tiptoed up just as a man was telling his fellow warrior about a dream, explaining in verse 13-14 that:

"'In my dream a loaf of barley bread
came tumbling down into the Midianite camp.
It hit a tent, turned it over, and knocked it flat!'

His companion answered,

'Your dream can mean only one thing—
God has given Gideon son of Joash, the Israelite,

victory over Midian and all its allies!'"

When Gideon heard the dream and its interpretation, he thanked God, worshiping Him. Then he returned to his own camp full of courage and woke his men, reassuring them that the Lord would help them be victorious (Judges 7:15)!

Per the Lord's instructions, Gideon divided his men into three groups of 100, giving every man a ram's horn and a torch covered by a clay jar. He told them to keep their eyes on him, following his lead.

When Gideon came to the edge of the enemy camp, he blew his ram's horn and broke his clay pot. Then all 300 men blew their horns and broke their jars. They held their blazing torches high in their left hands and their horns in their right hands, shouting in verse 20:

"A sword for the Lord and for Gideon!"

Each warrior stood bravely. Then the Lord caused chaos among their enemy and they panicked, fighting against each other with their swords. Those who were not killed fled as fast and as far as possible.

I could relate to the men who woke up disoriented from fear. Like me, when I first awoke from my dream, I was disoriented from fear.

I love that God encouraged Gideon *through* a dream. In turn, Gideon's story encouraged me *to get through* a dream. For me this was a gloomy, fear-ridden moment that became a **Glimmer**

of Glory. The Light of God's Word, through this story about Gideon's victory over fear, helped drive my fear far away.

I closed my Bible and smiled as I walked down the hallway back to bed. Pausing momentarily to gaze at my safe, sleeping beauty, who was still sucking her thumb, I whispered a peaceful prayer of thanks.

THE JOURNEY FORWARD:

Just as God's Word provided the perfect story at the perfect time, Scripture can do the same for you. God has great timing. He doesn't want you to face your fears without faith in Him. Don't have your fears place you facedown, rather face your fears down today. Rest in His love.

POPCORN

*I*magine the savory, scrumptious aroma of fresh theater popcorn laden with oodles of butter. I find popcorn to be irresistible. Movies always seem better with a bucket of it.

Here at the Wilt residence, we pop double monster batches the old-fashioned way on the stove in a kettle with oil. Even my daughter wants her own big bowl, as my five-month-old son reaches for it.

At our home, popcorn is a grocery staple like bread or milk because it is a nutritious snack. I don't think I've ever met anyone who doesn't like it. This love extends beyond the human race; even our fur babies beg and perform tricks for it.

RECENTLY WHILE WAITING FOR A BATCH TO POP, I WAS LEFT TO reflect on how much a kernel of popcorn has in common with faith. Let me explain.

If you apply heat to a kernel, it pops. That physical heat can be compared to the heat described as:

"the fiery trials of life."

If we persevere in faith, the outcome of those trials will be a blessing (1 Peter 4:12-14).

James gives us some serious food for thought concerning faith, explaining that it needs to be more than just words. If we see a friend in need, he tells us we need to do more than say hello. We need to provide for their needs.

He reminds us that faith without works is of little value (James 2:14-26). Likewise, a kernel of popcorn is of little value to the hungry snacker. You and I wouldn't dream of placing a bowl of unpopped kernels before our children or guests.

Together we are called to feed those who are hungry. Wouldn't you love to be as irresistible as buttery popcorn? I want my good deeds to be so numerous they pop the lid off others' expectations. Like a bowl that overflows spilling popcorn on the floor, I want my kindness to overflow and grace those around me.

In addition to being healthy, popcorn is a great value. A two-pound bag, which would provide over a bushel of popped corn, costs less than two dollars. As a poor pharmacy student, even I could afford popcorn. Likewise, our faith is of great value. Everyone can afford faith. It enriches our lives, nourishing us.

THE JOURNEY FORWARD:

Take time today to "pop" into someone's life. Be that delicious, nutritious pick-me-up! Listening to someone, if even for a few moments, may bring **Glimmers of Glory** to them. Offering a kind word could be so simple, yet so scrumptious to the starving soul.

On your journey forward today, can you treat yourself to a bowl of popcorn that's so full it is "running over and pouring into your lap" while you reflect on Luke 6:38:

"Give, and you will receive.
Your gift will return to you in full—
pressed down, shaken together to make room for more,
running over, and poured into your lap.
The amount you give will determine the amount you get back."

THE DISAPPEARING EIGHT BALL

They were bright and colorful. They made a special cracking noise as they bounced across the marble floor. And they were off limits, which made them all the more enticing. But they fit so perfectly in her little hands. Indeed, Alyssa found them to be irresistible.

They were Daddy's billiard balls.

As she hid under the pool table, she lined them up in a row all nice and neat. She admired the sound they made when she whacked them together. Then she had an exciting idea. Since they looked bright and colorful like her Easter eggs, she would hide them. It would be so great!

Why was Daddy so frustrated?

Why didn't he think it was fun to look for the balls?

He was talking very low and slow as he bit his lip asking: "Can you tell Daddy where you hid all the balls?"

She held his big hand and pulled him toward each of her hiding places. That was fun. But Daddy didn't want to jump up and down and clap when she found one. "You're s'posed to clap," she informed him with her hand on her hips and her brows furrowed.

Daddy wasn't much fun.

She found them all. All but one. Daddy wanted the ugly one. "Where did you hide the black one, Sweetie?" She did not remember. "The one with the eight, Honey?"

What was an eight? She was tired of looking for Easter egg balls. "I want to play something diffrant," she smiled, losing interest.

WEEKS HAVE DISAPPEARED AND MY HUSBAND'S BLACK BILLIARD ball has never reappeared. Despite hours spent looking in every conceivable place—short of removing every floor air duct—it seems to be permanently lost.

Have you ever lost one pivotal piece of a set that can't be individually replaced? For me it's a weekly occurrence to lose something, though it usually resurfaces. How many times in a month do you misplace your keys or your phone?

I'm a patient person when dealing with others, but I'm impatient with myself. And I dread looking for things. Perhaps it's because I don't like to waste anything—least of all, time.

A pet peeve of mine is to turn everything upside down and inside out in an all-out search. So today I asked God to help me find **Glimmers of Glory** in those maddening moments of searching for a lost receipt. This is what I found.

Even the time we spend trying to locate something is not time lost. While our feelings of aggravation increase, so does our opportunity to experience the joy that Jesus describes in His Parable of the Lost Coin.

In Luke 15:8-10 He tells the story of a woman who had ten coins...until one turns up missing. Ugh! So she turns on the brightest lights, looking everywhere until she finds it. And when she does, in excitement she calls her friends and neighbors to come over to celebrate her good fortune. Then Jesus tells us that's the kind of party God's angels throw every time one lost soul turns to Him.

After finding whatever I have misplaced (like a credit card), I feel a sense of joy and relief. At the Wilt Residence we do what I call a "happy dance." It's an arms-up-in-the-air, joyful jig with a hooping, hollering rhythmic chant thrown in for good measure. Anyone who knows me understands I take rejoicing to new heights (or new depths depending on what you think of my dancing and singing).

Although feelings may vary in intensity, based on the importance of the item, we can still better appreciate the sense of great joy that Jesus describes. In comparison to a sinner finding salvation through Christ, finding an eight ball is insignificant.

So when searching for something lost, can you let it remind you of the frustration that God must feel over His children who are lost? People are infinitely more important than things. Wouldn't you agree?

This is why the Lord is waiting to return. He wants to give everyone time to accept His gift of salvation, not wanting anyone to die without having heard the Good News. Ultimately, He wants all of us to spend eternity with Him in heaven (2 Peter 3:9). What Father wouldn't want His kids around?

THE JOURNEY FORWARD:

So next time you find yourself searching for *something* you have lost, can you pray for *someone* who feels lost? Ask that God will prepare their heart for the message of salvation?

Pray that God will grant you wisdom and courage, if you are to speak with them. And could you pray that His Spirit will provide the most appropriate words? Like me, you may find that searching for *something* that is lost may not be nearly as frustrating if you use the time to pray for *someone* who is lost.

So you may be wondering whatever happened to the eight ball. Well...it remains a mystery to this day. Thankfully my brother ended the search, when he arrived with a replacement ball as a Christmas gift for my husband.

ATTEMPTED AND PREMEDITATED

The headline says it all! M-U-R-D-E-R. Six letters combined into one word that shock us, searing our souls.

It seems to be a household word these days. Every week brings more horrific headlines. I cringe…but what can I do? As a working wife and mom of two, I am overwhelmed.

Today I read about a teenager whose father tried to kill him and I'm saddened. The details are unfathomable, as the father made his son participate in preparing his own slaughter.

What father would do this?

First, the boy was strapped down so that he could be executed. The plan was to then set his corpse on fire. This murder was premeditated.

The man had taken the boy from his mother and had traveled several days from their hometown. As a mother myself, I was so thankful and relieved to read that the boy actually lived through the ordeal, though I'm sure he was never the same. How could he be normal?

Would you believe me if I told you that the man has since become quite well known. You could read about him and about this now famous attempted murder online, as he was being tested and directed by God. Yes, really. He was the father of the Islamic, Jewish and Christian faiths.

His name was Abraham.

We can read about this twisted trial in Genesis 22. The unfathomable story is one that we have grown up hearing in church and Sunday school. But have we ever questioned: "Why did God test Abraham by asking him to sacrifice Isaac, his long-awaited son?"

While the motives between attempted sacrifice and attempted murder are certainly different, both result in death. What could a loving God have possibly had in mind?

Before the days of cinematography, God was bringing to life the profound docudrama that would take place centuries later when He allowed the sacrifice of His Son.

In the ten verses of Genesis 22:1-10, I counted five parallels between Isaac's near sacrifice and that of Jesus' complete sacrifice. Isaac–Abraham's promised son–was to be sacrificed on a mountain, just as Jesus–God's promised Son–was sacrificed on a mountain.

Abraham took two young men with him. Jesus had two young men with Him when He hung on the cross. Isaac carried the wood upon which he was to be sacrificed. Likewise, Jesus carried the wood upon which He was to be sacrificed. Just as Isaac's life was spared on the third day, Jesus came back to life on the third day.

Isaac probably sensed a deep solemnness as he and his dad walked. Keep in mind that Abraham was well over 100 years old at this point. He had longed for this promised son for nearly seven decades.

You know that Abraham had to be both feeble from age and frail from sorrow. Imagine waking up thinking: "This is the last time that I will eat breakfast with my son."

Then as they packed up their camp, Abraham may have been thinking: "This is the last time that Isaac will strap on his sandals."

The first time that a child takes their first step is joyous. The first time that a child puts on their own shoes is a milestone. Knowing that these simple activities are "lasts" surely beckoned tears.

Isaac knew only what he was told. He and his dad were traveling to offer a sacrifice to God on Mount Moriah. But as they neared their destination, Isaac was direct. In Genesis 22:7, Isaac asked the horrific question that must have pierced the heart of Abraham:

"But where is the lamb for a burnt offering?"

In agony, Abraham answered in verse 8:

"My son, God will provide himself a lamb."

Little did Abraham realize at the time that he had prophesied the birth of the Lamb of God Who would come to take away the sins of the world. In his desperation, Abraham had foretold not only of the birth but also of the sacrificial death of Jesus Christ.

It is difficult to comprehend Abraham's willingness to sacrifice his own son. It seems unthinkable, demented and brutal. How could Abraham love God seemingly more than his own flesh and blood?

I can't imagine being asked to choose between God or my children. But isn't that what God did when He allowed His Son to die for us? He chose us, letting Jesus be crucified.

Though God had the universe at His disposal, all the wealth of creation, and legions of angels, He had only one Son. God sent His perfect Child to suffocate...nailed naked to a tree.

In anguish, Jesus–Who had never known a moment without His Father–felt forsaken when He cried out in Matthew 27:46:

"My God, my God, why have you abandoned me?"

God heard. I feel certain He wept. What Dad wouldn't? Agony doesn't describe the torture both Father and Son knew that dark day.

They did it for you.

They did it for me.

It is an amazing gift.
An overwhelming sacrifice.
We call it grace.

THE JOURNEY FORWARD:

In Psalm 22, we can read about the despair the psalmist experienced, as he was the first to pen the question: "My God, my God, why have you abandoned me?" Through Christ, we can take comfort in the New Testament promise of Hebrews 13:5:

> "I will never fail you.
> I will never abandon you."

LIGHTNING AND THUNDER

How long has it been since you have lain awake during a loud storm? You see the flashes of lightning first, and then you hear the bellowing thunder. Truly God reflects His awesome power in nature. We see **Glimmers of Glory** in each flash of lightning.

Have you wondered why the light precedes the clap of thunder? Light waves (traveling at roughly 186,000 miles per second) are 100,000 times faster than sound waves. In short, we see the light...then we eventually hear the sound. In ancient times, philosophers such as Aristotle believed that thunder was caused by the collision of clouds. We now understand that thunder is caused by the sudden expansion of air in the path of the electrical discharge used by the lightning.[1]

THERE'S A LESSON TO BE GLEANED FROM BOTH LIGHT AND SOUND waves that applies to the time we spend reading God's Word. When we read, we first *see* the words. We may *see* an entire chapter each night.

But the real question is not *how much* we read or for *how long* we read. *Seeing* the print does not guarantee that we understand the truths, remember the message or comprehend the parables and prophecies.

Though visualizing the print is accomplished by the retina detecting variations in light wavelengths, *hearing,* in the Biblical sense, requires much more than the detection of sound waves. In Romans 10:17, we are reminded by Paul that:

> "So faith comes from **hearing**, that is,
> **hearing** the Good News about Christ."

Notice that Paul chose his words carefully. Faith comes by *hearing.* It takes longer to hear a clap of thunder than to see the flash of light, and it takes longer for our **heart** to truly **hear** His Word than it does to just see it. I'm slow, but hopefully it won't take me 100,000 times longer!

Together we can ask the Holy Spirit to help us, just as He promised in **John 14:26:

> "But the Comforter...shall teach you all things,
> and bring all things to your remembrance,
> whatsoever I have said unto you."

That's my prayer for us on our journey. That with the Holy Spirit's help we will not only see God's promises in His Word, but we will hear and remember "all things" we learn on our journey.

THE JOURNEY FORWARD:

Have you ever noticed that your eyes have lids so that you can close them, but your ears don't? Perhaps this is God's way of letting us know that it's best to be open to hearing.

Best of all, it's a recipe for joy, based on the truth of Proverbs 8:34:

"Joyful are those who listen to me."

Though your eyes may be shut, the next time a storm blows your way, let the thunder and lightning provide **Glimmers of Glory**.

---

1. Thomas, Tai "Thunder vs. Lightning" Stanford.edu http://large.stanford.edu/courses/2016/ph240/thomas1/ (Accessed March 3, 2019)

HELD HOSTAGE

 *T*ension brought tears. My daughter whimpered. The hostage lay perfectly still as if to plead, "Please come rescue me." No one exhaled.

What should I do? Now my daughter was wailing. Who would hear me if I yelled? We were facing a crisis, as Alyssa had hit the electric locks when she crawled out of the car.

Her "blankie" was held hostage in her car seat. I counted three...three sets of car keys. The dilemma was that all three sets were locked in the car. I could see the set on the front seat. There was a second set in my work tote and the backup set in my purse on the floor.

To borrow the lyrics from an old Hall and Oates love song, they were "so close, yet so far away." As I stood with my hands cupped to my eyes peering in the window, I gritted my teeth and asked for a **Glimmer of Glory**. Taking a deep breath, I thought of my husband. He would be shaking his head in dismay if he were standing beside me.

I reminded myself, I should count my blessings. Things could be worse. At least the car was in the garage, where it was a few degrees warmer than some freezing parking lot.

But that didn't change the fact that my daughter was ready to take her nap and she "needed" her blankie. Though it was torn from the many times it had been caught under the stroller wheels, thin from constant washings, and spotted with last night's spaghetti sauce, there was no substitute.

What's a mom to do?

WE ALL HAVE THINGS TO WHICH WE CLING. WHAT DO WE treasure most? Do we cherish objects? Do we rely upon crutches? Are we comfortable without our security blankets? Like...

Our makeup?

Our job titles?

Our accomplishments?

Our spouses?

Our habits?

Our kids?

Though we may not "need" a blankie as my daughter does, we do have legitimate spiritual needs. I personally need God's strength in times that I am weak (2 Corinthians 12:10). Truly, I would be wise to rely on God all the time.

My daughter takes her blankie with her everywhere, which reminds me of the verse that Paul penned, telling us in **1 Thessalonians 5:21 to:

"Prove all things;
hold fast that which is good."

My daughter has *proven* her blanket, and she literally holds fast to it, so much so that the inner batting is falling out. When she lays down, she pulls her blankie to her face and holds tightly to its corner, just as we are told to hold tightly to hope. God can be trusted to keep his promises (Hebrews 10:23). And the verse that follows encourages us to motivate others to reach out in love and kindness. These good works provide **Glimmers of Glory** to others. They may be just what is needed to show others that Christ is trustworthy.

In Christ we have hope. We know that the best is yet to come in heaven. Yes. There will be gloomy, frustrating days on earth when we lock our keys in the car and our toddler is frantic, but this trouble is momentary.

Just as my daughter needs the security of her tattered but proven blankie, we each need the security of knowing we are accepted by God through Christ. That hope is true. It's the Good News that provides comfort and strength, peace and joy. While our faith is comforting, it is so much more than a security blanket that children, like my daughter, cling to. Our faith is both secure and it saves! By **faith** we are saved through grace (Ephesians 2:8).

THE JOURNEY FORWARD:

As you end this day's journey, when you get in bed and cover yourself up with a blanket, rest in the secure promise that God will welcome you with open arms, when we run to Him for cover (Psalm 5:12). He rescues us...much more skillfully than I rescued my daughter's blanket using a wire coat hanger to pop the lock.

A ROSE & ITS THORNS

When my husband and I were dating, he rented a small house near The University of Kansas Medical Center. To say it was modest was an understatement. But he was a bachelor with medical school debt, so it served him well.

I was paying off my debt from pharmacy school when he asked me to be his wife. Having both been raised in frugal families, we appreciated the small splurges in life. Miniature roses were one such splurge.

At a gas-station-turned-flower-shop, on occasion David would buy me two dozen multicolored, miniature roses. They cost him $9.99. I loved them because I loved him. For many, roses are a traditional way to say, "I love you."

To this day, baby roses bring such rich memories of two poor people who loved one another dearly. What do you see first when you look at a rose? If I had to guess, I'd say that you named the colorful petals.

Petals are the most beautiful, most fragrant and most delicate part of the flower. They could be equated to the love we experience in our life. Days filled with love are days filled with beauty and fragrance. They are days that we treasure.

1 CORINTHIANS 13 PROVIDES US WITH MANY CHARACTERISTICS OF love. So it's no surprise that we hear this chapter read at weddings. How many of the characteristics of love can you name? For the record, let's count. According to the New Living Translation love is:

1. patient
2. kind
3. never jealous
4. never boastful
5. never proud
6. never rude
7. never demands its own way
8. never irritable
9. never keeps record of being wronged
10. never glad about injustice
11. always rejoices when truth wins out
12. never gives up
13. never loses faith
14. always hopeful

15. always endures through every circumstance

Have you ever counted the number of petals on a rose? There are just about as many characteristics listed as there are petals. The more years I am married, the more I am convinced that roses and marriages have much in common.

While individual petals can remind us of the characteristics of Biblical love, the thorns are the negative characteristics that we each bring to the relationship.

Have you ever heard someone who is admiring a rose comment–not on the beauty of the flower–but on the ugliness of the thorns? I never have. Why? The focus is concentrated on the lovely petals.

Roses are the most popular flower to be given to express love. When I accept them from my husband–not only is each petal a reminder of love–but it is a reminder to focus daily on *the positives…the petals.*

Why would I purposefully focus on the thorns?

Yes. My husband is imperfect. He comes home tired and cranky after a fourteen-hour day. But focusing on his irritability will not bring me joy. As the old adage goes, "Your glass is either half empty or half full." The same can be said of relationships.

Roses have thorns. Spouses, even parents, siblings and co-workers, have imperfections. You choose what your focus will be and remain positive. It is good to know where the thorns are located. Then with some care, they may be avoided.

In *Philippians 4:8, St. Paul gives us some excellent guidance telling us to focus our minds on things that are:

"true, noble, reputable, authentic, compelling, gracious—
the best, not the worst; the beautiful, not the ugly;
things to praise, not things to curse."

Then, in *verse 9, he shares an incredible promise that is
meant for us as much as it is meant for the people in Philippi,
saying:

"God, who makes everything work together,
will work you into his most excellent harmonies."

We all could use lives that are filled with "most excellent
harmonies" rather than clashing discords. In *The New Living
Translation Bible,* these verses conclude with Paul advising:

"Think about things that are excellent and worthy of praise...
and the God of peace will be with you."

So today I will choose to see the fragrant good in people,
choosing not to focus on their thorny shortcomings.

While no one is perfect and without thorns, no one deserves
to be purposefully hurt by thorns. Thorns on roses are not used
as weapons. If someone is deliberately hurting you, know that
this is not love. Also know that you are worth so much more
than thorns.

Never having met you, how can I know your worth? Because
Christ wore a crown of thorns and died on the cross, because He
loved you and me. If we are valuable enough for our Father to

allow His Son to die for us, we are valuable beyond measure. You were bought with an extraordinary price (1 Corinthians 7:23). Let no one tell you that you are less worthy.

THE JOURNEY FORWARD:

On your journey forward today, can you focus on one positive trait of your spouse, a thorny friend or family member? Why not provide a **Glimmer of Glory** and brighten their day, sharing your positive thoughts? The compliment will probably be as welcomed as a delicate rose. And the best part is that it will be remembered longer than any flower could survive.

The next time you give or receive a rose, can you focus on what God says Biblical love is like, based on the list we found in 1 Corinthians 13?

STUBBORN STAINS

*T*oday I wore a buttery yellow blouse with what looked like chocolate on the right shoulder; it was mid afternoon before one of my nurses told me about the spot. I'd like to think it was food, but with a newborn and toddler both in diapers, who knows?

Being a nursing mom who hasn't gotten a good night's sleep in months, I don't have the energy to be embarrassed. As I write, I am more focused on the fact that my son is starting to eat some semi-solids, which means I get to sleep thirty minutes longer each morning. Yahoo!

Garrett wears the largest portion of a jar of Gerber's Baby Food®. Full-body splash guards would be more effective than bibs. Maybe I am just particularly sloppy, or my son particularly fast at grabbing. It's probably some of both. Regardless, *food time* is *fun time* at the Wilt residence.

We all like to eat. While I enjoy carrot cake straight from the oven, Garrett enjoys strained carrots straight from the jar. Which brings me to the issue of stains and how hard they are to remove from a kid's clothing. I need help on so many levels.

AS I THINK BACK TO MY BLOUSE, IT SEEMS TO ME THAT STAINS ARE like bad memories. It's the residue that's left behind in my mind after I forgive someone who has wounded me with their hurtful words or attitude.

While I do want to fully forgive, I find that the ugly memory is still hanging around–much like an ugly stain. And just like the stain, the memory often pops up in the worst place at the worst time. Can you relate?

The first step in forgiving is to take the offense to God. Likewise, the first step in laundering is to take the clothes to the washer. But just washing clothes doesn't always completely remove the dirt. Similarly, forgiving doesn't always completely remove the hurt.

Do you struggle with fully forgiving like I do?

I find that forgiving can be hard, especially when it's a recurring offense or, even worse, when the person doesn't seem sorry. If they're family or a friend, how do we deal with the hurt?

How do we balance forgiveness with wisdom in our interactions? While trust is earned, forgiveness is freely given. This reminds me of the time Peter asks Jesus how many times we're to forgive someone. When inquiring if we should forgive an offender seven times, Jesus replied in Matthew 18:22:

"Seven! Hardly. Try seventy times seven."

Hmm. I'm no mathematician, but I do know that 70 x 7 = 490. This means that someone could commit the same offense every day for nearly 1½ years. And I am called to forgive every single day. Of course, this is Jesus using hyperbole to make the point that we need to continue to forgive.

But how do we balance this forgiveness with wisdom so that we are not a modern-day doormat? Personally, I have to take it to God in prayer, because I have that question often.

I do know that if someone is inflicting harm, you need to protect yourself and your family. But what about those less extreme offenses that just threaten to steal our joy? Those are the things that I struggle with most.

Then in Matthew 18:23-35, Jesus told a parable about a king who decided to collect the money that he was owed. One man was in debt the equivalent of roughly $100,000. Since he couldn't pay, the king ordered him to be sold as a slave along with his wife, his children and his property. This was common in Biblical times, when nearly forty percent of the Roman Empire was enslaved.

The indebted man was distraught, throwing himself at the king's feet, begging for the chance to pay him back. The king was merciful. Being touched by his plea, he generously erased his debt completely.

After the man left the king totally absolved of his $100,000 debt, he went to find his neighbor. The man owed him ten dollars. He seized him by the throat and demanded payment immediately.

When the poor neighbor threw himself at his feet and begged for the opportunity to pay him back, he had no mercy. Rather he had his neighbor arrested and jailed.

When others observed this interaction, they were rightfully angry and went to the king. Then the king summoned the ungrateful man saying in verse 32-33:

"You evil servant!
I forgave your entire debt when you begged me for mercy.
Shouldn't you be compelled to be merciful
to your fellow servant who asked for mercy?"

The king was justifiably mad, giving him the punishment that he imposed on his indebted neighbor. Jesus concluded in verse 35 saying that's how His Father will react to anyone who doesn't "forgive unconditionally," anyone who asks for mercy.

Honestly, it will take me a lifetime to master *unconditional forgiveness*. I don't have all the answers and I'm far from perfect when it comes to forgiving. But on our journey, I am learning from God daily.

God wants me to leave my disappointments and hurts with Him. He can shoulder the burdens that I can't...without becoming weighed down and depressed. I know that God always listens and understands.

Amazingly, as I learn about forgiving others, I am learning about God's nature and finding **Glimmers of Glory** in offering grace.

For me, working full time with two kids in diapers and a husband who works eighty hours every week is a trial. But in *Luke 23:33-34, we read about a more excruciating trial in Jesus's life:

> "When they got to the place called Skull Hill,
> they crucified him, along with the criminals,
> one on his right, the other on his left. Jesus prayed,
> **'Father, forgive them; they don't know what they're doing.'"**

As Jesus hung naked for everyone to see, He cried this prayer; the soldiers were deciding who won which pieces of His clothing. They showed no compassion and no remorse. In fact we learn a few verses later that they mocked Christ.

Even one of the criminals who hung next to Him joined in ridiculing Him. But the other criminal saw Jesus's innocence and defended Him, asking that Jesus remember him when He arrived in heaven. Jesus said that He would do more than just remember. He would welcome this man into His kingdom (Luke 23:43).

I'm blown away that Jesus forgave the soldiers who didn't *ask* for forgiveness. He even forgave the criminal who didn't *earn* forgiveness. And I am even more amazed to know that when we ask, God fully forgives our sins.

The price has been paid by Jesus. It's in the past. We don't have to keep petitioning God for forgiveness. He doesn't keep remembering and reminding us of our failings to punish us. In Hebrews 8:12, He reassures us:

> "And I will forgive their wickedness,
> **and I will never again remember their sins**."

Now to me this sounds unfathomable that an all-knowing God would *choose to forget my sins*. In my humanness, this is very difficult for me to comprehend. Are we also called to this level of forgiveness?

If so, how can we remove offensive, hurtful stains from our memories? Humanly speaking, I find it's impossible. Which brings to mind Matthew 19:26, where Jesus explains grace, saying:

> "Humanly speaking, it is impossible.
> But with God everything is possible."

Years ago I saw a cartoon depicting this concept of God's agape love, forgiveness and conscious choice to forget. It showed a man dumping his sins remorsefully into the "Sea of Forgetfulness." The most poignant sketch in the cartoon was the sign on which was printed in bold letters: "**No Fishing Allowed**."

Once we have confessed our offenses, God forgives us. He chooses not to dwell on the hurt, as it has been covered by

Christ's sacrifice made in love. He focuses on Christ's *obedience*, not our *disobedience*.

Call it a mystery if you like. I don't know what to call it… other than amazing grace.

This doesn't mean that we are free to continue to offend God or others. If we truly are contrite, our goal will be to break sin's cycle. The Greek word for repent is "metanoeo," which means "to change one's mind."

Blouses can be replaced. And while a stain is an annoyance, it's certainly not an offense that begs forgiveness. But there are hurts that we each experience in life that do mar us. The stain on my blouse reminds me that holding onto hurts, refusing to forgive, leaves a lingering, ugly stain. Fully forgiving others, as Christ forgives us, leaves us stain free, spotless and glimmering.

THE JOURNEY FORWARD:

On our journey forward today might we choose not to focus on the hurt? Forgiving the offense is grace for the offender…but it's grace for us too. The next time I pray *The Lord's Prayer,* I'm going to pray that He helps me be more like Him when I forgive others.

As I think about it, praying in advance for God's help in forgiving is a bit like pretreating a stain. My Mom always taught me to pretreat my laundry. Sometimes in haste, I skip this step. I have a long way to go, but I know He can help me, as He is the Master at stain removal and redemption.

UNCLE DON

AND BRACH'S® CHOCOLATE STARS

*T*en years ago today my Uncle Don died from bone cancer. He's the only uncle I grew up knowing, as he lived straight down 12th Street on Marshall Avenue near Lawson Park in Mattoon.

The last time I saw him, he was smiling and happy to share some hosta plants from his garden for me to transplant into my yard in Kansas City. He was always kind and generous.

When I was a kid, he shared his chocolate with me and my siblings. Then as an adult, he shared tips on life and gardening. He had no intention of leaving his garden or this earth anytime soon.

You see, he was just diagnosed with osteosarcoma, yet he was ready and willing to fight. He had recently retired, after years of being a mailman. Wanting to enjoy life, to rest in his backyard with sweet tea and to coach Babe Ruth Little League, Uncle Don had planned his retirement.

Even though Jesus was his Coach and Friend, my uncle did not want to die...not just yet anyway. I find that I can feel similarly. Do you?

True, those of us who know the Lord have no reason to fear death.

True, we Christians are told by Paul to pray for Christ's return.

True, heaven is going to be better than our most glimmering moments here.

True. True. True. There are many reasons to look forward to eternity. Yet it is difficult to talk with a relative, a friend, or a patient who has little time left in their bodies.

What do you say and what do you avoid saying? Chances are you and me, like so many others, don't want to say anything wrong. We really don't know what to say as words fall woefully short.

I believe our presence says more than any words. And we can never go wrong with a loving smile, a meal or a gentle hug. Funny thing, despite all the aggravations of our aging bodies, we hate to think about parting with them, diseased as they may be.

THERE IS ACTUALLY A REASON WE WANT TO HANG ON TO OUR bodies and stay here on earth. God originally made us to live forever, but then we chose sin, which leads to death. As an alternative to death for our sin, God sent Jesus, offering salvation (1 Corinthians 15:45). Jesus explained to Nicodemus that we need to make a decision to follow Him for our spirits to be "born again."

When Nicodemus asked how we can physically return to the womb, Jesus replied in John 3:5-6:

> "I assure you, no one can enter the Kingdom of God
> without being born of water and the Spirit.
> Humans can reproduce only human life,
> but the Holy Spirit gives birth to spiritual life."

Born again implies that at one time our spirits were alive. Being born again restores us to our *original* state…before *original* sin.

However, the story doesn't end there. In Romans 6:23 we read that the "wage" of sin is death. This refers to the death of our physical bodies. As Christians the assurance that we have is that the death of our spirits will not occur.

Our spirit and our resurrected body will live forever in heaven (1 John 5:13). That's where my uncle is now. And someday I will see him.

Even still…I miss him.

As a child one of my sweetest memories of Uncle Don was the sweet secret we shared. In the bottom drawer of his clothes chest, he always had a bag of Brach's Milk Chocolate Stars® hidden for our visits. He would wink and motion for Kathy,

Brian and me to scamper silently past Aunt Martha in the kitchen.

When he would ask us how many stars we wanted, we were so excited, we could hardly swallow our giggles! Of course, we wanted as many as our little hands could hold. What kid wouldn't?

Though I don't see bags of Brach's chocolate stars often these days, I do see stars in the night sky and often think of Uncle Don and smile.

He was a **good** mailman.

He was a **good** person.

He was a **good** husband.

He was a **good** father.

He was a **good** uncle and…

He was a **good** Little League coach, who died much too young.

Now some may say it is a coincidence that Lawson Park–just steps behind Uncle Don's backyard–hosts the World-Wide Little League Babe Ruth World Series. This is a BIG deal for a small town like Mattoon.

And some folks may think it is a coincidence that Mattoon has been given such an honor. But I know it's no coincidence. Uncle Don may not have had time on earth during his retirement to help organize this, but he apparently has had time during his heavenly retirement.

As star athletes and big names in baseball like Cal Ripkin converge on my small home town, I grin and gaze at **Glimmers of Glory** in every star in the sky.

THE JOURNEY FORWARD:

My Uncle Don always called me "Precious," so today I am comforted by the promise of **Psalm 116:15:

> "Precious in the sight of the Lord
> is the death of his saints."

On my journey forward, rather than focus on my loss, I'm going to buy some Brach's chocolate stars to share with my family. Most importantly, I'll share memories of my uncle, who called me "Precious." Can you too find *God moments* in the *gloomy moments* surrounding the loss of a loved one?

UNLOCK THE DOOR

TO BLESSINGS

Since my children have been born, my husband and I rarely go out for a grown-up date night. When we are able to steal away, the children's Godparents babysit. They have such fun.

Alyssa and Garrett are made to feel like the queen and king of Kansas City. We order pizza and–best of all from my daughter's perspective–she gets soda pop. With all the sugar, she is wound and ready to give her Godparents a run for their money.

Of course when Mom and Dad are gone, the unforeseen happens. Such was the case last night. My daughter had just learned how to lock doors, which made her feel very powerful and grown-up. She practiced her newfound talent with one flaw in her demonstration. She was inside the bathroom with no light and her pizza was outside.

Now, normally all you have to do is turn the knob and the

lock pops open. But my daughter's greasy little hands just couldn't accomplish the job. The task was made tougher by the fact that she was only using one hand; the other was grasping a flashlight to chase away the darkness.

Her dear Godmother urged her to put down the flashlight and use both hands to turn the knob. Alyssa was too afraid to let go of the things that brought her comfort.

Her tears turned into wails as her Godfather frantically searched for a screwdriver to pop the lock. The whole episode took only minutes, but it made a lasting impression on my daughter. She is a bit more careful in her locking escapades.

As Sharon recounted the story, I was reminded of Jesus's words in *Revelation 3:20 when He explains:

> "Look at me. I stand at the door. I knock.
> If you hear me call and open the door,
> I'll come right in and sit down to supper with you."

I have seen this scene painted by William Holman Hunt. He thoughtfully created the door with a knob on only one side. Jesus was on the outside, like Alyssa's Godmother.

The choice to allow Jesus access to our hearts and lives is ours. We each have a free will to make decisions that impact our life here and eternity later. So often those with wealth rely solely on their 401k's for their future, trusting in their money alone to save them. Finances are not a replacement for faith.

Those who don't know Christ don't open the door of their hearts. They don't trust Him. The same was true when my daughter was locked in the bathroom. Had she only trusted her Godmother and put down the flashlight, with two hands Alyssa could have opened the door.

THE JOURNEY FORWARD:

Have you ever opened the door to Christ, laying down your will? Now for the harder question: what areas of your life may still be closed off to Him? On our journey forward today, can you lay down your fears and let Him in the darkest rooms of your heart? You will find He brings **Glimmers of Glory** with grace.

TRUST

T-R-U-S-T. Five letters. It's easy to spell and even easier to lose, but hard to earn.

If you make a quick mental list of those whom you trust, who would be on it? The first five on my list are my husband, my parents and my siblings.

I can also say I trust God. The more I have gotten to know Him over the years, the more I trust Him. How about you? When bad things happen, do we believe that God has our best interests at heart?

Do you and I implicitly trust that God is in control? Initially, we may not see the good. That's when I remind myself that I don't see the whole picture. Can I share a raw example with you?

Tonight I sat down at my computer. Although it was late, I was so close to completing this book, I ached to print it out, as I was curious to see how many pages there would be. However, I quickly realized that something had gone terribly wrong.

Over half of the pages were nowhere to be found. I opened every window, file and drive possible. Still they were missing. You can imagine my anxiety. As I tried to remain calm, my stomach churned uncontrollably.

I thanked God that I had printed out a copy of each chapter as I had finished it. But every page would need to be retyped. As a working mother of two, running a household, the thought of this was overwhelming.

My goal was to print the first complete copy of the book for my dear friend–Cyndi Scarlett–before she left to go back to Africa. She was home for the holidays and I wanted to share a copy with her for her staff. They needed the encouragement.

Now how could I possibly meet this deadline? It seemed impossible. I trusted that this manuscript was God's work. This was His project and I knew He could and would provide.

I prayed for peace…for wisdom. Then I remembered a friend who was out of work and needed extra money. Perhaps I could pay him to retype the pages. I trusted that God could bring good even out of loss (Romans 8:28). Then I reminded myself to be thankful, things could be much worse.

Have you ever lost something that you thought you had saved on your computer? If you have, you know the feeling and understand the frustration.

At moments like these a Scripture that I memorized years ago from Proverbs 3:5 comes to mind. It directs me to:

> "Trust in the Lord with all your heart;
> do not depend on your own understanding.
> Seek his will in all you do,
> and he will show you which path to take."

I find that it's easier to trust God when life is predictably good. But when life is botched and bad, can we trust Him then?

We are told by Jesus that rain will fall on both the righteous and the unrighteous. (Matthew 5:45). Then we are told by St. John that we **will** face **many** trials (John 16:33).

When I lost most of this manuscript, my first reaction was to ask God **how** and **why** this happened. Yet I know that the better question is, **what** does He want to teach me in the trial?

Tests of faith or trials will come as assuredly as rain. And we know that just as rain is needed to sustain life, trials are needed to refine faith (James 1:3-4). So though most of my book is missing, I trust Him to bring good from this trial.

THE JOURNEY FORWARD:

On your journey forward, when you encounter a computer glitch—whether it is monumental or minute—be encouraged that while you may not always trust technology, you can always trust God.

While both trial and trust share the same starting consonant and number of letters, they share much more than that. Trust can sustain us during a trial when we truly believe that God can take what could harm us to accomplish good (Genesis 50:20). Trust can trump any trial and even transform us! My computer glitch became a blessing to my friend needing to earn extra cash.

HIS TURN

Growing up,
my grandma was the greatest.
Grandpa was okay.
You see,
I really didn't know him well...
then.

I remember Grandma's "chicky bird" eggs,
the lake of butter on her mashed potatoes,
but best of all, her back scratches.
Grandma always had the scratchiest skin,
but the kindest hands.

Grandpa and Grandma,
Bernard and Mary.

They lived down the block,
across the street
and over the train tracks.

Those tracks are long gone,
but the memories remain
of my grandparents,
rocking
and waiting
on the front porch.

For us–
Kathy, Lisa, and Brian–
to trot
up the steps
and to the door.

Grandpa always had the screen door locked.
Why?
Who knows?
Habit had him hopping
to harmonies
only he could hear.

Mattoon,
the Nales' hometown,
wasn't exactly a torrent of crime.
It was quiet

and cozy
to its 18,000 inhabitants.

Grandpa and Grandma
had lived for decades at
208 North Twelfth
with siding made of steel,
a one-bedroom house
modest yet rich.

Perhaps
greater than any gift
my grandparents ever gave us
was the gift of their testimony
to the covenant
of marriage.

No. Their lives weren't easy.
Their relationship had its share of thorns
but they persevered.
And the result?
A couple in love
in their nineties,
seemingly inseparable.

But now,
Grandma has gone to her heavenly home
and Grandpa forgets...

or does he?
He reads
and rereads the same newspaper.

He is a man of small stature.
His heart is large.
It is a heart
that has softened with age,
with years and trials.

I know
only tales
of the younger years
when some say
he was harsh.

Today,
I see a man of great patience,
a man filled with gratitude,
a man full of kindness,
a soul filled with light
and love.

Tears are common.
Joy is evident.
Hugs are welcomed.
Great-grandchildren are bounced
on his knee.

With amazing virility,
our family agrees,
Grandpa,
skin toughened and tanned,
has a softened heart.

He was born
when the century turned.
We wonder
when will it be
his turn
to go home?

⁓

*T*ruly, my grandfather was blessed with old age. I remember in his eighties, when he was baptized and came to know Jesus more personally. Much like ocean waves, time has a way of wearing the rough and jagged edges off a heart. But not everyone is going to have the luxury of a century to become fervent about their faith.

The question then is how long will we wait before reaching out to Jesus as a Friend? He can do so much more than just save us. He can lead us through the gloomy days that have sorrows and the losses. He can comfort us and blaze the trail today.

Waiting to become serious about our faith is a gamble. A wager that is oftentimes silently lost between the paychecks and promotions...the debts and doubts.

Yes. There have been people on their deathbeds who have made peace with God and their family. They have said their good-byes to those they love and hello to a Savior they really never knew.

But why wait to reach out to a Father Who loves you right now? He doesn't want you to die to meet Him. He wants to meet you today!

So I have to ask, do you know where your soul and spirit will go when you breathe your last breath here on earth? God wants you to come home to Him. His love letter is addressed to each of us. It's an invitation to heaven found nestled in John 3:16-18:

"For this is how God loved the world:
He gave his one and only Son,
so that everyone who believes in him will not perish
but have eternal life.

God sent his Son into the world not to judge the world,
but to save the world through him.
There is no judgment against anyone who believes in him."

Salvation saves us from judgement (Psalm 103:10-12; Isaiah 38:17; Isaiah 44:22; Micah 7:19; Hebrews 8:12; 1 John 1:7). It is a gift given freely. It is granted regardless of merit or "years of service" (Ephesians 2:8-9).

This is communicated in the Parable of the Vineyard Workers in Matthew 20:1-16, who were paid the same full day of wages despite their different hours of service. When Jesus explained the parable, he shared that the vineyard represents the kingdom of Heaven.

No matter how late in life a person comes to Him, **everyone who comes will be saved.** Though my grandpa came to know our Lord after eight decades, he is in heaven just like my grandma, who knew Jesus much earlier.

The gift of God is eternal life through Christ (Romans 6:23). Have you grabbed that gift? He's waiting for you to unwrap it now and begin your journey with Him. **Glimmers of Glory** can start now.

THE JOURNEY FORWARD:

At the age of 103, nearly a decade after I wrote this poem about my Grandpa, it was "His Turn" to journey to heaven. Though he couldn't tell you his age, he could tell you he was born in 1900 at the turn of the century!

And while he couldn't spell or tell you the names of all his great-grandchildren, he could still smile and spell "M-I-S-S-I-S-S-I-P-P-I" when asked by one of his great-grinning-grandkids!

FOR SUCH A TIME AS THIS

S ince this is the last mile of our journey together, it seems only fitting to glance back and reflect before we cross the finish line. Our goal was to discover **Glimmers of Glory** in the gloomy moments.

While God could still appear in a burning bush or send prophets, He uses the Bible to speak to us in modern days (Hebrews 1:1-2). This is why so much of our journey in these pages look to Scripture, where we learn about Him as the Word made flesh. And it is why we are blessed as we read our Bibles.

When I glance back at my formative years, I am reminded that we all have hopes and dreams of what we will be when we grow up. My maiden name was Nale, pronounced like a metal nail. My Dad always chuckled, saying: "The Nale family was as tough as nails."

While I sometimes feel more fragile than tough, I will say

that my dad taught us to be strong and resilient by his example. He also taught us to be novel.

While most little boys wanted to be firemen or policemen, my baby brother wanted to be a "pop man." He enjoyed playing with keys and he loved to drink soda pop. Even then he thought logically and decided to combine the two passions in his life. I have to smile because today Brian is an executive for a beverage company.

Time has brought many changes. I had almost forgotten about my aspiration to be a cheerleader. Then I found the half-sheet of powder blue construction paper that my first-grade teacher used to document my goal. On the left side of the paper Mrs. Beasley glued my smiling picture and underneath she printed: "Lisa wants to be a cheerleader."

To the right she spelled out my name vertically, placing an adjective beside each letter:

- **L**–Loving.
- **I**–Intelligent.
- **S**–Smiley.
- **A**–Always willing to help others!

God knew even back then that I would be a cheerleader–not for a professional sports team–but for my family. As moms, don't we cheer for our children every day? They may attend schools where God's name is forbidden, but make no doubt about it, God is there with them.

When I was five, I dreamed about owning a pair of pom-

poms. Never did I dream God would have me write books and speak to cheer others on in their spiritual journeys. I was struggling to master phonics. My "R's" sounded like "W's" as I would repeat for Mrs Beasley, "Wonnie Wabbit Wuns Waces." The harder I tried, the harder my classmates laughed.

Funny thing, if we ask God to use us, He will. He directs our steps. Today I can correctly pronounce my "R's," and I can also attest to God's generosity, giving me God moments to brighten the gloomy moments of life.

GOD CAN REVEAL HIMSELF IN **GLIMMERS OF GLORY** AND GOD moments, in stories and sometimes even in acrostics. I love books with happy endings, so as we near the end of our journey I want to share a Cinderella story about a Jewish heroine named Esther.

The book of Esther is the only book in the Bible where God's name is excluded. It never appears...not once. But make no mistake, God was right there with His children–the Hebrew nation–even when they were discouraged and exiled.

Interestingly, there are some that say they have found God's name embedded in acrostic form during pivotal times in the book of Esther. And while the most credible scholars do not make note of these acrostics, all scholars do agree that the book of Esther is a real life example of God's divine care and guidance in a gloomy period of Jewish history.

Likewise, I have experienced God's care and guidance in my

life during gloomy trials. In this book He has given us **Glimmers of Glory** in our daily experiences...messages of love and encouragement to brighten and lighten our days.

We read in the book bearing her name that Esther keeps her people from being exterminated by an enemy named Haman. With great courage and devotion, she has the help of her adoptive father–Mordecai. Like any great adventure, there are unpredictable, perilous points in the plot.

On our journey we too have had many twists and turns encountering **Glimmers of Glory** in the gloomy moments of our lives. He has shown Himself to us, just as He did to Esther and the Jewish nation exiled in a foreign land. Although she and her people felt forsaken, God worked through Esther to protect them.

Their story is set at the winter residence of the Persian emperor–King Ahasuerus. Not only is the book entertaining and exciting, it also explains the background and meaning of the Jewish festival of Purim, which celebrates God's delivery of His people from extermination.

The book of Esther is one of only two books in the Bible named after a woman. (The other is the book of Ruth.) It's found in the Old Testament, sandwiched between the books of Nehemiah and Job.

The author is unknown, just as the story of this Jewish queen is unknown to many. So why would I choose to focus on Esther? Because I believe we have much in common with her. Like you and I, Esther had an imperfect life. She had a difficult past, having been orphaned. She was married to a difficult man. She dealt with difficult people in a difficult country during difficult times. Can you relate?

Esther was adopted, just like we have been adopted into God's family. And when her adoptive father asked for her help, she showed up. Every day of our journey, you too have shown up.

Esther's strong story can be our story. Esther is both brave and beautiful; she is strategic and smart, exemplifying a wise woman. In Esther 4:14, her adoptive dad came to her and explained that she was needed, saying:

> "Who knows if perhaps you were made queen
> **for just such a time as this?**"

Throughout the remainder of the story, we see Esther use her position as queen to intercede to save her people. While I am not a queen, I am a wife, a mom, a daughter, a sister and a friend. Most importantly, I am a Christian.

Daily, my adoptive Father asks me a similar question saying: "Who knows if perhaps you were made…a wife, a mom, a daughter, a sister, a friend and a Christian…for such a time as this?"

We can touch the lives of others, showing them God's saving grace daily. Our children depend on us to teach them about God, to walk in faith, to exemplify kindness and to never stop encouraging them to bring God glory.

We teach our family how to love unconditionally by caring

for them. You and I are needed in our community to display God's mercy and grace. God can use you right where you are:

"for just such a time as this."

How do I know that? Ephesians 2:10 tells us that God has us where he wants us at this very moment in our lives. Through Jesus He wants to shower grace and kindness on us so that we can share it with others.

He wants us to trust Him enough to let Him save us, starting right now in this life. He created each of us to join Him in the work He does. What can you do today to love others sharing the Good News with "your people"?

THE JOURNEY FORWARD:

As we prepare to end our journey, can you prayerfully ask God to heighten your perception to His spiritual truths? Though His name never appears as part of the written text and He is not a character in the story of Esther, He shows up in people when He is most needed.

Likewise, we can be the people who show up for others when they most need God. We can be **Glimmers of Glory** to the world, especially in those gloomy moments when others need Him most! You can be a rainbow for someone after a rainy trial!

So it seems fitting to share this acrostic that can serve as a banner of sorts to encourage us to keep the faith and run the race. None of us have arrived. We are on this journey together as women of faith. Truly:

G – *God's*

L – *Love*

I – *Illuminates*

M – *Mundane*

M – *Minutes and*

E – *Experiences* if only we

R – *Remember* to

S – *Seek*

O – *Our*

F – *Father's*

G – *Guidance* while

L – *Living*

O – *Our*

R – *Remaining*

Y – *Years.*

RAINBOWS AFTER THE RAIN

We started our journey reflecting on rainbows. So I had to smile today when a friend shared a picture of a rainbow that was so vibrant it took my breath away beckoning me to pause. It was a double rainbow and doubly special, because it was such a rare sighting where she lives. Diana lives in the desert of Arizona.

Isn't that just like God to show up in the most unlikely of places? Rainbows in the desert. The thought makes me giggle. It's so like Him to share unexpected **Glimmers of Glory** just to see if we're watching.

We learned that the birth of a rainbow begins with a trillion tiny droplets of rain becoming reflectors of light…creating perfect prisms.

On our journey, we learned that *colorless* light enters one individual droplet. Then it exits bent and broken into the seven splendid colors of the spectrum. This broken light becomes beautiful light.

In our lives and on our journey we have looked at bent and broken moments asking God to show us **Glimmers of Glory**. When we slowed down, He showed up. When we kneeled down, He lifted us up.

We learned that rain can birth spectacular rainbows and stormy trials can birth spectacular growth. We looked to God to make us both whole and holy. Indeed, rain can nourish life, just as trials can nourish faith.

So with our faith strengthened, let's turn to an unlikely book in the Bible written by a man known as the weeping prophet. Jeremiah penned all five chapters of Lamentations. It is a *short* book about a *long* trial.

Living in exile, God's chosen people were bent and broken. The book of Lamentations is nestled between the prophetic books of Jeremiah and Ezekiel. Honestly, it's easy to miss between pages that stick together. Who really wants to read a book that's filled with gloom and doom?

I prefer happy endings. So why would I choose to rest on the last steps of our journey at this vantage point, overlooking a deep ravine of despair? Because the book of Lamentations is all about remembering. And rainbows prompt us to do just that... to remember.

The first rainbow to debut on this earth was sent by God after The Flood to remind us of His promise to never again destroy the earth with water (Genesis 9:15-16). God is a kind

Father. He didn't want us to fear each time a droplet fell thinking a flood would drown us.

Likewise, God doesn't want us to panic when trials drop into our lives like raindrops. Yes. Trials are gloomy and difficult, but He is beside us....even if we are bent and broken, "exiled in a foreign land" like God's chosen people were in the book of Lamentations.

Maybe you feel exiled and lonely right now. We each have times of loneliness. May I ask, in what ways have you felt exiled on your faith journey? Though I have never been exiled from my home, I have experienced the pain of being exiled from a close relationship. I have been exiled from a job. I have felt humiliation and despair. But God has not left me bent and broken...or alone.

He pulls you and me from the "mud and the mire" (Psalm 40:2). He loves us and chooses us (John 15:16). Because of that love, He wants us to remember that...

He is trustworthy...*even when spouses are not.*

He is faithful...*even when friends are not.*

He is just...*even when bosses are not.*

He is kind...*even when kids are not.*

He is patient...*even when you are not. And*

He loves you...*even when you don't feel lovable.*

As we rest on the ledge looking to Lamentations, I must tell you that God's *chosen* people *chose* sin and *rejected* Him. They were unjust and mistreated the poor. They made poor decisions that led to idolatry...then defeat...then to slavery...and ultimately to poverty.

Sometimes we too make poor decisions. Sometimes we become enslaved...

to jobs...

to habits...

to desires...

to lifestyles...

to relationships...

to our pride.

I won't name them all. I couldn't possibly.

Just as in the book of Lamentations where God wanted the Hebrew nation to remember to choose Him, God wants us to remember to choose Him. For this reason Jeremiah wrote in a way that was memorable.

Lamentations is written as verse, which is easier to remember, rather than as prose, which is random, making it more difficult. According to Bible-History.com, "the first four poems are arranged in an acrostic form with each containing 22 verses which correspond with the 22 consonants of the Hebrew alphabet. In chapter 3 each letter of the Hebrew alphabet is allotted 3 of the 66 verses which comprise the poem. Some conclude that the reason for this was because Israel had sinned from beginning to end (A-Z, or in the Hebrew, aleph-tav)."[1]

In ancient times, before books were readily available, information was passed from generation to generation by word of mouth. God made it a point to *simplify* this *difficult* message:

Separation from Him brings pain. And while pain can lead to tears (our own form of rain), we're told not to become lost in our tears but rather to relax in His love (1 John 4:18).

So as we come to the last bend in this trail, kick off your hiking boots and find a soft place to sit...to lean back and rest... to ponder this last prayer. It's one that Paul prayed for each of us in Ephesians 3:16-19:

"I pray that from his glorious, unlimited resources
he will empower you with inner strength through his Spirit.
Then Christ will make his home in your hearts as you trust him.
Your roots will grow down into God's love and keep you strong.
And may you have the power to understand, as all God's people,
how wide, how long, how high, and how deep his love is.
May you experience the love of Christ,
though it is too great to understand fully.
Then you will be made complete
with all the fullness of life and power that comes from God."

We are made complete by His love. Lacking nothing. We can rest in Him. Solid in faith. Rock solid. Radiant. Unshakable. Beautifully bent, as we lean on Him. Beautifully broken into splendid splashes of color.

THE JOURNEY FORWARD:

Have you ever noticed that rainbows and remember start with the same consonant and share the same number of letters? I did today. **Rainbows** do help us **remember**.

So on your journey forward, can you remember to hike close to God? Don't leave His side...not for a day. No doubt, we will still experience rainy trials and tears, but there will be rainbows too. When you feel gloomy, will you search for **Glimmers of Glory**?

It's a choice...and a challenge. I'm up for both. Are you? Please, take some pictures along the way so when our paths cross again in heaven, you can tell me the story that birthed each glimmering rainbow.

---

1. "Lamentations in the Bible" Bible-History.com https://www.bible-history. com/links.php?cat=42&sub=884&cat_name=Bible+Books&subcat_name= Lamentations (Accessed March 3, 2019)

ABOUT THE AUTHOR

Lisa Wilt is an inspirational speaker and author of multiple books including Windows of Wonder, which was awarded the gold medal by Illumination Book Awards. These awards honor the year's best new titles written and published with a Christian worldview.

Lisa's radio show, W.O.W. Words, airs daily to lighten the load for those on the go. Her podcasts and blogs can be found on Life885.com. Lisa is founder and president of *Rx for the Soulful Heart*, a ministry to encourage weary people and worthy ministries, with all proceeds from her speaking and books being donated to charity. You can visit her at LisaWilt.com and learn more.

For over 32 years Lisa has worked full-time as an award-winning pharmacist in community pharmacy and the pharmaceutical industry. By grace, Lisa and her husband—a physician—have two grown children who have followed in their medical footpaths. Of all her accomplishments, the title that most defines her is CHILD OF GOD. As her family will tell you, Lisa's singing is dreadful but her banana bread is delightful.

Made in the USA
Columbia, SC
17 February 2020